"Boykoff has a deep understanding of how the Olympic Movement operates behind the scenes and, equally important, as a former athlete, he understands the immediate need for enhanced rights for athletes."
Rob Koehler, Global Athlete

"Boykoff succinctly holds a magnifying glass to the structures of power entrenched in the Olympics while also holding space for communities continually left out of its iconic five rings."
Courtney M. Cox, University of Oregon

"Invaluable in exposing the long-standing problems with the Olympics, the persisting erosion of leadership in the Olympic Movement, and the consequences and impact for all involved."
Harry Edwards, Professor Emeritus, University of California, Berkeley and Olympic Project for Human Rights

"Across the globe, people are demanding, 'NOlympics Anywhere'. Boykoff's thorough research helps us understand why. A must-read for sport fans who care about justice."
Satoko Itani, Kansai University

The status quo is broken. Humanity today faces multiple interconnected challenges, some of which could prove existential. If we believe the world could be different, if we want it to be *better*, examining the purpose of what we do – and what is done in our name – is more pressing than ever.

The What Is It For? series examines the purpose of the most important aspects of our contemporary world, from religion and free speech to animal rights and the Olympics. It illuminates what these things are by looking closely at what they do.

The series offers fresh thinking on current debates that gets beyond the overheated polemics and easy polarizations. Across the series, leading experts explore new ways forward, enabling readers to engage with the possibility of real change.

Series editor: George Miller

Visit **bristoluniversitypress.co.uk/what-is-it-for** to find out more about the series.

JULES BOYKOFF is the author of five previous books on the Olympic Games, most recently *The 1936 Berlin Olympics: Race, Power, and Sportswashing* (Common Ground, 2023), *NOlympians: Inside the Fight Against Capitalist Mega-Sports in Los Angeles, Tokyo, and Beyond* (Fernwood, 2020), and *Power Games: A Political History of the Olympics* (Verso, 2016). His writing on the Olympics has appeared in academic journals such as the *International Review for the Sociology of Sport*, *Sociology of Sport Journal*, and the *International Journal of the History of Sport*, and in media outlets like the *New York Times*, *The Nation*, and the *Guardian*. He teaches political science at Pacific University, USA.

WHAT ARE THE OLYMPICS FOR?

JULES BOYKOFF

First published in Great Britain in 2024 by

Bristol University Press
University of Bristol
1–9 Old Park Hill
Bristol
BS2 8BB
UK
t: +44 (0)117 374 6645
e: bup-info@bristol.ac.uk

Details of international sales and distribution partners are available at
bristoluniversitypress.co.uk

British Library Cataloguing in Publication Data
A catalogue record for this book is available from the British Library

ISBN 978-1-5292-3028-4 paperback
ISBN 978-1-5292-3029-1 ePub
ISBN 978-1-5292-3030-7 ePdf

Cover design: Tom Appshaw
Bristol University Press uses environmentally
responsible print partners.
Printed and bound in Great Britain by CPI Group (UK) Ltd,
Croydon, CR0 4YY

FSC
www.fsc.org
MIX
Paper | Supporting
responsible forestry
FSC® C013604

For Kaia Sand and Jessi Wahnetah

CONTENTS

LIST OF FIGURES AND TABLES

Figures

Tables

ACKNOWLEDGEMENTS

A big thank you goes to series editor George Miller for the initial invitation to write this book. Thanks also to the anonymous peer reviewers for their astute insights and helpful feedback. Thank you to Vaarunika Dharmapala at Bristol University Press for wonderful editorial assistance. Here's to the library staff at Pacific University for their assistance throughout this project, especially Jennifer Bosvert, Michelle Lenox, Christine Remenih, Justyne Triest, and Jerica Tullo. Thank you to the Dean's Office at Pacific University for financial support and to Mia Tenditnyy for reliable research assistance. Thanks be to friends and colleagues for their intellectual generosity: Shireen Ahmed, David L. Andrews, Molly Boykoff, Ben Carrington, Meg Eberle, Kent Ford, Chris Gaffney, Tina Gerhardt, Robin Hahnel, Satoko Itani, Cedric Johnson, Ximena Keogh Serrano, Sang-hyoun Pahk, Tania Peña, DeVon Pouncey, Neal Sand, Susan Schoenbeck, Sven Daniel Wolfe, and Dave Zirin. Finally, infinite thanks to Kaia Sand and Jessi Wahnetah for your moxie, your hilarity, your love.

INTRODUCTION

The Olympics Games are a massive, hugely popular festival of sport that platforms the world's best athletes. Many Olympians are household names. Think of Jamaican sprinter Usain Bolt, US swimmer Michael Phelps, German speed skater Claudia Pechstein, or Japanese wrestler Saori Yoshida. Or, dipping into history, there's Romanian gymnast Nadia Comăneci, Cuban boxer Teófilo Stevenson, Norwegian figure skater Sonja Henie, and US track legend Jesse Owens.

Simultaneously, as the world's biggest sports, media, and marketing event, the Games are an entrenched cultural referent and an economic juggernaut that nets enormous revenues for the International Olympic Committee (IOC), the powerful group based in Lausanne, Switzerland that oversees the Olympics and selects their host cities. When it comes to the Olympics, there's a lot going on beneath the shimmering surface. Thinking through five illustrative snapshots can help us better understand where the Games stand today.

Snapshot 1: The IOC broke fresh historical ground when, in 2017, it announced two host cities at once: the IOC chose Paris to host the 2024 Summer Games and Los Angeles to stage the Olympics in 2028. The two cities were originally vying for the 2024 Games, but after high-profile bid withdrawals from Boston, Budapest, Hamburg, and Rome, the IOC made the unusual dual declaration. In LA, the path was relatively smooth, but at a heated subcommittee meeting that preceded the vote, one City Council member assured skittish Angelenos who were raising critical questions about the Olympics that the mega-event would 'create jobs and weed out poverty and put Los Angeles on the map'. In August, when the Los Angeles City Council voted unanimously to authorize Mayor Eric Garcetti to sign a host-city contract with the IOC, the council chambers transformed into a sporty coronation, with US Olympic icons like swimmer Janet Evans, track star Carl Lewis, and diver Greg Louganis taking turns at the microphone to champion the cause. After the vote, Mayor Garcetti convened council members, staffers, Olympians, and Paralympians for a victory photo.[1]

Snapshot 2: In recent years, the IOC has embraced sports like snowboarding and surfing to attract younger audiences. When the IOC announced the inclusion of breakdancing as an Olympic sport at the Paris 2024 Games, the South African comedian Trevor Noah joked on *The Daily Show*, 'The Olympics is getting desperate again'.[2] Noah implied that the IOC's move to stay relevant in sport's increasingly competitive attention economy came across as clumsy pandering to lure young people, an awkward attempt to lacquer hipness onto the Games.

Snapshot 3: A few months ahead of the rescheduled Tokyo 2020 Olympics, a poll in Japan found that 83 per cent opposed staging the Games amid the COVID-19 pandemic. When the public pressured Japan's Prime Minister Yoshihide Suga to further postpone the Games, he admitted that the host-city contract granted the power to cancel or postpone solely to the IOC. The IOC ignored public opinion and pressed ahead with the Games, even though Japan had barely commenced its vaccination programme. COVID-19 rates in Tokyo increased dramatically during and after the Games, while more than 800 people tested positive for COVID-19 inside the 'Olympic bubble'.[3]

Snapshot 4: In April 2022, the *Guardian* revealed that John Coates, an IOC vice president and the outgoing president of the Australian Olympic Committee, wrote a letter of recommendation effusively praising *himself*, asserting that it was 'hard to think of anybody better qualified in the world of sport' to be added to the 2032 Brisbane Olympics organizing committee. Previously, Coates helped re-write IOC rules to make it possible to allocate the Olympics to cities whenever they could lock in local leaders and well before any significant opposition could organize. Brisbane, in Coates' home country of Australia, took advantage of this new rule 11 years in advance of the Games it will host in 2032.[4]

Snapshot 5: As global pressure mounted on sports bodies around the world to embrace – or at least positively acknowledge – the zeitgeist of athlete activism that was sweeping the world, IOC President Thomas Bach doubled down on the IOC's longtime mantra that the Olympics are not political, writing that the IOC 'is strictly politically neutral at all times' and 'the Olympic Games are not about politics'.[5]

The IOC's stiff insistence of its own apoliticism has become an Olympic tradition of sorts.

These five snapshots tell us a lot about the current state of the Olympic enterprise. First, the IOC is willing to adapt its practices and rules – selecting two host cities at once, one 11 years in advance when the typical lead time had been seven years – when it sniffs opportunity. Also, after the photo-op in Los Angeles, when Mayor Garcetti headed to the podium to praise the bid team's efforts, his plaudits were muffled by jeers from angry activists chanting 'Halt the Games!' The 21st century has seen a surge of anti-Olympics activism in response to Olympic patterns and controversies that will be examined in Chapter 3. In 2019, anti-Games activists from around the world convened in Tokyo for the first-ever transnational anti-Olympics summit where they shared knowledge and resources. They met again at the University of Paris in summer 2022 to strategize against the Olympic machine (see Figure 0.1).

Second, the Olympics have seen a sharp downturn in primetime viewership, with the Beijing 2022 Winter Games securing the all-time lowest ratings in the television era. At the same time, digital streaming and social media impressions saw significant increases, especially among younger audiences.[6] Because broadcaster rights comprise 61 per cent of the IOC's revenues, these trends are no trivial matter.[7] The changing tides of viewership, swishing atop demography's ever-shifting tectonic plates, help explain the IOC's embrace of sports like skateboarding and

Figure 0.1: Activists attend the second-ever transnational anti-Olympics summit at the University of Paris in May 2022

freestyle skiing aerials: the IOC is making a calculated gamble on its fiduciary future.

Third, the IOC talks in glowing, even inspiring, terms about its mission and guiding principles, but consistently privileges its own interests, even etching vital advantages for itself into host-city contracts. Had Olympic brass listened to the credible public-health concerns of jittery citizens in Japan and cancelled the Games, the IOC would have forgone billions in revenues, jeopardizing its profit margins (even as it collected insurance money, to be sure). The group tends to conflate its own interests with the welfare of the wider world. Under the spell of this logic, the Games must always go on. This tendency has spurred accusations that the IOC practises the art of self-aggrandizement masquerading as social concern.

Fourth, the chutzpah pumping through Olympic circles is legendary. Back in the 1990s, when Sydney was bidding on the 2000 Summer Olympics, John Coates, who was leading the city's bid team, admitted offering US$35,000 to two IOC members – one from Uganda and the other from Kenya – the day before Sydney defeated Beijing in a nail-biter 45–43 vote. Coates even stated that 'to a large extent' Sydney won the vote because it 'bought the Games'. Despite openly admitting what happened, he was cleared by an independent auditor of any wrongdoing, fuelling the notion that IOC members enjoy congenital impunity, making it difficult to rein in five-ring corruption.[8]

Finally, from the beginning of the Olympics, when plucky French aristocrat Baron Pierre de Coubertin launched the multi-sport event in 1896, the IOC has claimed that the Games transcend politics. And yet, the IOC's brand of apoliticism has long been deeply political; Olympic history is brimming with politics. After all, the IOC staged the 1936 Summer Games in Berlin with full knowledge that Adolf Hitler and the Nazis were amassing power while weaponizing the Games against Jewish people by instituting an 'Aryans-only' policy within German sports organizations. The IOC allowed an all-White apartheid team from South Africa to compete until it grudgingly banned the country in the 1960s in response to worldwide pressure. For two decades, the IOC's president was Juan Antonio Samaranch, an unrepentant functionary for the fascist Franco regime in Spain. The IOC's conspicuous tolerance for tyranny is political, as when it allowed Beijing to host the Olympics even when the actions of the Chinese government clashed mightily with key principles in the Olympic Charter. Even the structure of the Olympics energizes political nationalism: Olympians march in the opening ceremony by country when they could just as easily do so by sport.[9]

After Russia unleashed a full-scale invasion of Ukraine only four days after the Beijing 2022 Winter Olympics closing ceremony, both Bach and Coates of the IOC demanded the exclusion of Russian athletes from international sport because of politics and war (although Bach and the IOC later backtracked).[10] Then, Bach further waded into politics when he shared the stage and posed for photos with Ukrainian President Volodymyr Zelenskyy.[11] In July 2022, Bach met with UN Secretary General António Guterres where, according to the IOC's social media, they 'discussed the geopolitical situation'.[12] In short, the IOC uses apoliticism as a shield to ward off criticism and to avoid prickly issues. In doing so, the group neglects the fact that claiming neutrality can mean supporting oppressive forces. In reality, sports are politics by other means.

What Are the Olympics For? charts the rise of the Olympics into the behemoth that it is today as well as the controversial downsides that arrived with the mega-event's growth. The Olympics thrum with a paradox: they are still enormously popular globally and yet the Games elicit vigorous dissent in host cities – and prospective host cities – as the pitfalls of the event have

Figure 0.2: The IOC and the UN have a long-standing relationship

UN Secretary General António Guterres (left) shakes hands with IOC President Thomas Bach during a press conference in Pyeongchang, South Korea before the 2018 Winter Olympics on 9 February 2018.

become more widely known. Increasingly, calls have emerged from around the world to reform the Games so that they better align with the lofty, admirable principles enshrined in the Olympic Charter.

Along the way, I examine the evolving role of Olympic athletes, both their triumphs and their tribulations. On one hand, the remarkable performances of Olympians are what make the Games special. On the other hand, athletes are increasingly voicing concern over physical, mental, and sexual abuse, and they are uniting to collectively express their grievances around equity and human rights. In theory, the Olympics are for athletes – the IOC often proclaims that it is 'Putting Athletes

First'.[13] In practice, though, athlete wellbeing often comes closer to last, and Olympians themselves are increasingly speaking out about it.

Sports are never simply sports. Sport occupies a distinct 'social place', as scholar Chen Chen puts it, that is shot through with politics even as the managers of sport regularly hoist the flag of apoliticism. The 'ghost of capitalism', Chen writes, plays a vital role in the organization of sport, including the Olympic Games.[14] The Olympics have long been riding the line between their perceived destiny and potential demise. This book helps explain why and, through illuminating the Games' historical lineaments, paves a path for a more just Olympic future.

1
HOW DO THE OLYMPICS WORK TODAY?

Olympians, everyone agrees, are what make the Olympics special. Czech gymnast Věra Čáslavská was an Olympic athlete who was an inspiration both in and out of competition. Over the course of three Olympics spanning 1960 to 1968, she amassed seven gold medals and four silvers. She was a crowd favourite at the 1968 Mexico City Olympics, and not just because she chose the 'Mexican Hat Dance' as the musical accompaniment for her final floor performance. The political context in 1968 stoked her popularity: Čáslavská outshone archrival Soviet gymnasts only two months after the Soviet Union invaded Czechoslovakia to snuff out the 'Prague Spring', a democratic uprising that aimed to break free of Soviet control.[1] While on the medal stand, Čáslavská caused a furore when she made an unequivocal, if subtle, political statement, dipping her head in silent protest during the Russian national anthem, a symbolic act of anti-imperialist defiance.

Prior to the Olympics, Čáslavská trained in hiding under suboptimal conditions. The Czechoslovak National Olympic Committee nearly withdrew from the 1968 Games, but managed to send a 100-member Olympic squad to Mexico.[2] Čáslavská paid a price for her principles. After her act of dissent, the Soviet-compliant government in Prague forbade her from travelling abroad or competing in gymnastics. But years later, after the fall of communism, Čáslavská became the head of the Czech National Olympic Committee as well as the eighth female member of the International Olympic Committee (IOC).[3]

Figure 1.1: Czech gymnast Věra Čáslavská

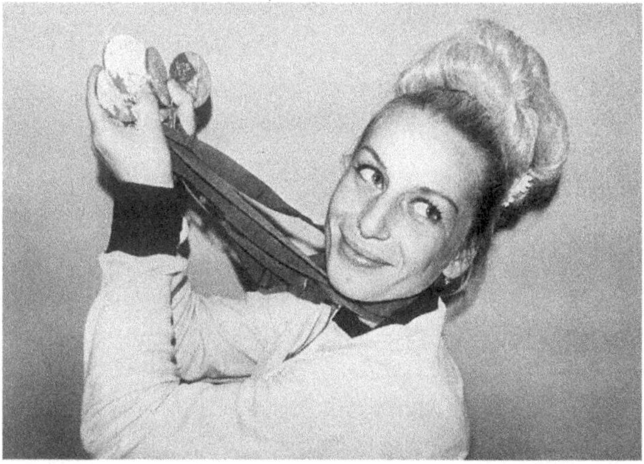

Věra Čáslavská won numerous medals at three Olympics between 1960 and 1968. She made a political statement when on the medal stand at the 1968 Olympics, dipping her head in silent protest during the Russian national anthem.

More than five decades after Čáslavská's success in Mexico City, US gymnast Simone Biles demonstrated the power of choosing *not* to compete in order to protect her physical and mental health.[4] With a combined 37 Olympic and World Championships medals, Biles is one of the most accomplished gymnasts of all time. But at the Tokyo 2020 Olympics, she was seized by a case of the 'twisties', a dangerous mental block whereby a gymnast's spatial awareness evaporates mid-performance. Biles chose to pull out of the competition. 'I have to do what's right for me', she said, 'and focus on my mental health and not jeopardize my health and my well-being'.[5] Her decision sent an important message to the world that there is more at stake than winning and losing, than medals and podiums. US President Joe Biden recognized this when he conferred the Presidential Medal of Freedom on Biles, making her, at age 25, the youngest person ever to receive the honour.[6]

In different ways, both Čáslavská and Biles capture the spirit of what Olympic founder Baron Pierre de Coubertin called 'Olympism'. The Baron wrote, 'Olympism is a state of mind that derives from a twofold doctrine: that of effort, and that of eurythmy'.[7] Eurythmy meant a life in harmonious balance, a 'divine harness' inherited from ancient times 'that is properly proportioned'.[8] Coubertin asserted:

> The primary, fundamental characteristic of ancient Olympism, and of modern Olympism as well, is that it is a *religion*. By chiseling his body through exercise as a

sculptor does a statue, the ancient athlete 'honored the gods.' In doing likewise, the modern athlete honors his country, his race, and his flag.[9]

Coubertin viewed Olympism as 'an *aristocracy*, an *elite*', albeit an 'aristocracy whose origin is completely egalitarian', based on hard work and sporting merit.[10]

Both Čáslavská and Biles achieved eurythmy: finding 'properly proportioned' balance on and off the terrain of sport. They also embodied the spirit of the Olympic Creed, derived from Coubertin himself: 'The important thing in the Olympic Games is not winning but taking part, just as in life, what counts is not the victory but the struggle.'[11] To be sure, the Baron would not have revelled in their success. For him, 'the true Olympic hero' was 'the *individual adult male*'. As will be discussed in Chapter 2, he adamantly opposed women's involvement in Olympic sport. 'I do not approve of women's participation in public competitions', he opined. 'At the Olympic Games, their role should be above all to crown the victors, as was the case in the ancient tournaments.'[12]

Nevertheless, the contemporary Olympic Movement has embraced both Olympism and women's participation. The IOC projects that the Paris 2024 Summer Olympics will be the first Games with 50 per cent female participation.[13] The Olympic Charter expands Coubertin's vision of Olympism, bringing it up to date. 'Olympism is a philosophy of life, exalting and combining in a balanced whole the qualities of body, will and mind', it states. 'Blending sport with culture and education, Olympism seeks to create a way of life based on the joy of effort, the educational value of good example, social responsibility and respect for universal fundamental ethical principles.' The IOC adds that '[t]he goal of Olympism is to place sport at the service of the harmonious development of humankind, with a view to promoting a peaceful society concerned with the preservation of human dignity'.[14]

The structure of the Olympic system

Based in Lausanne, Switzerland, the IOC is a non-governmental organization and self-proclaimed 'supreme authority' of the Olympic Movement.[15] It sits at the centre of the Olympic universe, and is orbited by National Olympic Committees (NOCs), International Federations (IFs) of sport, Organizing Committees of the Olympic Games (OCOGs) in each host city, National Sports Federations (NFs), and corporate broadcasters and sponsors.[16]

NOCs promote Olympism in their respective countries, run Olympic qualifier events, and are typically subsidized by the federal government of the territory they represent. NOCs are not only responsible for developing high-performance sport in their territories, but also for curating educational programmes that proliferate Olympic ideals. They oversee the training of sports administrators and select potential Olympic bid cities that can enter the race to host the Games. NOCs must maintain their autonomy from governments, choosing their own leadership, although NOCs are required under the Olympic Charter to include among their ranks all IOC members who hail from their country. At the time of writing there are 206 IOC-recognized NOCs, outnumbering the 193 United Nations member states, with the IOC accepting territories like Hong Kong and Puerto Rico, even though they are not UN members.[17]

IFs are the global governors of a particular sport (or several sports); for instance, the World Curling Association manages curling while the Fédération Internationale de Football Association, or FIFA, oversees football (soccer), beach football, and futsal. These non-governmental organizations are responsible for standardizing the rules for the Olympic sports they oversee. IFs regulate and manage their sports at the Olympic Games. They often bundle member NFs into continental confederations.[18] In the Olympic Charter, the IOC formally recognizes 28 IFs governing sports in the Summer Olympics and another seven IFs overseeing events in the Winter Games.[19] Three IFs preceded the creation of the IOC – the Fédération Internationale de Gymnastique, founded in 1881, and two IFs created in 1892: the International Skating Union and the Fédération Internationale des Sociétés d'Aviron (today, World Rowing) – while the others surfaced after the modern Olympics emerged.[20]

OCOGs are impermanent bodies created by an NOC and governmental authorities to organize a particular Olympic Games. OCOGs are usually public bodies, as with the Paris 2024 Organizing Committee, although sometimes they have significant private dimensions and leadership, as with the Los Angeles 2028 Olympics. The first time an OCOG arranged the Olympics was the 1908 Games in London.[21] The IOC monitors OCOGs, often through a body called a 'Coordination Commission' that is headed by a prominent IOC member. The Olympic Charter dictates that an OCOG must 'have the status of a legal person in its country' and include in its executive body any IOC members from the country where the Games are being staged as well as the president and secretary general of the host country's NOC.[22] After the Olympics conclude, OCOGs close their accounts, issue reports, and disband. For instance, the Tokyo 2020 Organizing Committee dissolved in June 2022, less than a year after the Games concluded after being postponed a year due to the COVID-19 pandemic.[23]

NFs perform the domestic role of IFs in individual countries, assembling sports clubs and issuing licences. NFs can be formally acknowledged as domestic leaders for their sport by both their respective IFs and NOCs. Olympic scholar Jean-Loup Chappelet describes NFs as 'national umbrella organizations for clubs within a given sport'. He adds that '[t]heir role with respect to the Olympic Games is to supply their NOC with athletes in their sport, who could participate in the Olympics if they achieve a minimum qualifying standard set by the IF'.[24] The Olympic Charter states that all national federations that are formally linked to the IFs that oversee Olympic sports should be included in the composition of their respective NOCs and that, at minimum, five IF-affiliated NFs must be included in an NOC.[25] An example of an NF is the Athletics Federation of Nigeria, which oversees track and field in the country.

Finally, television broadcasters and corporate sponsors have emerged as a crucial source of income for the IOC, contributing more than 90 per cent of its revenue: 61 per cent from broadcasters and another 30 per cent from corporate partners, according to the organization's 2021 annual report.[26] The first Olympic television coverage – albeit on delay – occurred at the 1936 Winter Games in Garmisch-Partenkirchen, Germany. Months later, the opening ceremony for the 1936 Berlin Summer Olympics was televised live in Germany. The Rome 1960 Summer Games were the first to be televised live across Europe; those Olympics were transmitted via delay to Canada, Japan, and the US.[27] Big media companies fork over hefty sums to the Olympic Movement for broadcast rights. Television revenues in Rome reached nearly $1.2 million ($12.4 million today, adjusted for inflation); that figure climbed to $1.6 million ($15.7 million today) at the 1964 Tokyo Summer Olympics.[28] Broadcast rights for the postponed Tokyo 2020 Games netted $3.1 billion for the IOC.[29]

Meanwhile, sponsor revenues were also on the rise. Prior to the 1980s, OCOGs raised corporate-sponsor funds, as when Tokyo 1964 organizers scored $1 million from an 'Olympia' cigarette brand (a move the IOC disapproved, subsequently banning tobacco sponsorships).[30] The 1976 Montreal Games featured a patchwork of more than 600 sponsors. This changed with the 1984 Los Angeles Olympics where organizers limited the number of official sponsors and required them to contribute a minimum of $4 million in cash or in-kind goods. Thirty-five corporations signed on, including behemoths like Coca-Cola, General Motors, Levi Strauss, McDonald's, and United Airlines. The IOC swiftly realized that this was the path towards financial stability. It created 'The Olympic Programme' (TOP) – launched at the 1988 Seoul Summer Olympics and the 1988 Winter Games in Calgary and later becoming 'The Olympic Partner Programme' of today – whereby select sponsors contribute millions in exchange for the exclusive use of the Olympic symbol. OCOGs are allowed to secure additional domestic sponsorship revenue, so long as it doesn't encroach on the IOC partners' commercial turf.[31] At the Tokyo 2020 Olympics, domestic sponsors contributed a record $3.3 billion.[32] TOP sponsors contributed $532 million in 2020 and $835 million in 2021.[33]

The International Olympic Committee, its regulators, and the five-ring money shuffle

The IOC describes itself as 'a catalyst for collaboration between all parties of the Olympic family'.[34] Its main job is to facilitate and help stage the Olympic Games. Founded in 1894 as the 'International Committee for the Olympic Games', the IOC initially comprised of 15 of Coubertin's hand-picked confidantes.[35] The Baron viewed the original IOC as 'three concentric circles'. The first was 'a small nucleus of active and convinced members' who made the big decisions. The second was 'a nursery of members of good will who were capable of being educated'. Third, there was 'a façade of more or less useful men whose presence satisfied national pretensions while giving some prestige to the group'.[36] This tripartite system essentially describes the IOC in the 21st century. Under President Thomas Bach, the IOC has concentrated power in its Executive Board and smaller 'Future Host Commissions' of no more than ten IOC members, while the larger body increasingly wields less direct power.[37]

The IOC has been headquartered in Lausanne, Switzerland since 1915, where it enjoys exemption from income and wealth taxes and streamlined access to work permits for foreign staff. During its 125th anniversary year in 2019, the IOC christened a fully self-financed building for its 500 employees towering over the Château de Vidy at a cost of around 190 million Swiss francs.[38] (The new headquarters caused a kerfuffle when, amid the pricey construction in Lausanne, the IOC rejected Rio 2016 organizers' plea for assistance with millions in debt accrued through staging the Games amid political and economic turmoil in Brazil.)[39] Lausanne has, over the last century, become an Olympic hub, with numerous IFs relocating there to secure easier access to the IOC and to take advantage of favourable tax laws.[40]

Since its creation, the IOC has had just nine presidents, all but one from Europe (see Table 1.1). Today, IOC presidents are elected via secret ballot by all members and serve an eight-year term, with the possibility of one four-year renewal. IOC members are added through co-optation: nominated by a current member and approved by the wider body. IOC members do not represent their country of origin; rather, they represent the IOC in Olympic matters. Scholars John Horne and Garry Whannel assert that '[t]he IOC remains a club based on the eighteenth-century aristocratic notions of membership associated with a gentlemen's club'.[41] The IOC began admitting women in 1981. By 2024, of 106 members, 44 were women. Of the 41 honorary members, two were women. The IOC also had one 'Honour Member', the late Henry Kissinger of the US.[42]

IOC members are not paid, but are eligible for $7,000 in administrative costs each year and receive a per diem – or 'indemnity' – of $450 on days when they attend meetings. Executive Board members and Commission Chairs receive $900 for each meeting day. All this

Table 1.1: Presidents of the International Olympic Committee

Name	Country of origin	Years of presidency
Demetrius Vikelas	Greece	1894–1896
Pierre de Coubertin	France	1896–1925
Henri de Baillet-Latour	Belgium	1925–1942
J. Sigfrid Edström	Sweden	1942–1952
Avery Brundage	United States	1952–1972
Lord Killanin	Ireland	1972–1980
Juan Antonio Samaranch	Spain	1980–2001
Jacques Rogge	Belgium	2001–2013
Thomas Bach	Germany	2013–present

comes alongside perquisites like top-shelf hotels, sumptuous meals, and high-quality transportation. The IOC president resides gratis in the Lausanne Palace Hotel and in 2021 received €275,000 to cover his costs.[43]

The IOC Executive Board, which has become especially influential under current IOC President Thomas Bach, was formed in 1921 and today contains the IOC president, four vice presidents, and ten additional members, all of whom are elected via secret ballot for four-year terms.[44] Various commissions, both standing and ad hoc, have increasingly taken on high-profile roles, from the Athletes' Commission – comprised of and elected by Olympic athletes to represent the interests of Olympians – to the Medical and Scientific Commission, which oversees issues relates to doping and athlete health.

In 1999, the IOC created an Ethics Commission after jaw-dropping allegations of corruption enveloped the 1998 Winter Olympics in Nagano and the 2002 Salt Lake City Games. In clear violation of spending limits, Nagano bidders lavished an average of $22,000 on 62 IOC members to entice their votes. Moreover, after the Games, Nagano Olympic officials incinerated their records.[45] Salt Lake City bidders created files on individual IOC members – noting their preferences and predilections – and then engaged in breathtaking bribery: almost 1,400 separate expenditures totalling nearly $3 million.[46] Congolese IOC member Jean-Claude Ganga secured more than $250,000 worth of gifts: his mother-in-law received a knee replacement, his wife got cosmetic surgery, and he underwent treatment for hepatitis. The son of another IOC member, Bashir Mohamed Attarabulsi of Libya, received tuition to attend Brigham Young University and a local community college, plus $700 monthly payments. Salt Lake City bidders also handed out cash.[47] The Ethics Commission, created in the wake of these allegations, submits its findings and recommendations to the IOC Executive Board, which has the final say on whether rules violations have occurred and how they should be dealt with. As such, Olympic scholars have concluded that '[t]he Ethics Commission cannot be considered as an independent body'.[48]

In recent decades, two high-profile organizations have emerged to regulate the Olympic sphere: the Court of Arbitration for Sport (CAS) and the World Anti-Doping Agency (WADA). Formed in 1983 by the IOC, CAS's main job is to resolve disputes by applying and interpreting the regulations of sport governing bodies, whether international or national. Based in Lausanne, it runs satellite offices in New York and Sydney, and sets up temporary courts in Olympic cities to settle urgent issues that arise. As an arbitration tribunal, CAS deals with two primary areas: commercial contracts and disciplinary matters, thereby building up global sports law created by judges, also known as *lex sportiva*.[49] Scholars have criticized CAS as a self-regulating legal system that operates autonomously, outside the purview of established national legal orders.[50] Increasingly, human-rights concerns are falling into the court's docket, leading some to argue that the court needs to reform to be more nimble, relevant, and just.[51]

With a mandate to promulgate, propagate, and enforce doping regulations, WADA was founded in late 1999. The goal was to centralize and implement the IOC's doping strategy, creating a one-stop-shop designed to dissuade athletes, doctors, and sport administrators from using or condoning performance-enhancing drugs. For decades, the scourge of drugs had been threatening the Games' profitability and damaging athletes' health. WADA is funded by the IOC, IFs, and NOCs as well as states that have signed onto the UNESCO International Convention Against Doping in Sport of 2005. WADA periodically updates its list of banned substances and coordinates with national anti-doping agencies to test athletes on an ongoing basis.[52]

For many spectators, what is most alluring about the Olympics is their audacious impracticality, with thousands of athletes from multiple sports converging from around the world to compete in one place. But this also makes for an expensive affair. A lot of money is swishing through the Olympic system. In the Olympic cycle spanning 2017 through 2020–2021, the IOC brought in $7.6 billion in revenues. The IOC emphasizes that it reinvests 90 per cent of its revenues back into the Olympic system – around $4.2 million each day – redistributing funds through various programmes designed to develop sport and support athletes around the world. The other 10 per cent goes towards IOC operations.[53] Alongside this, an avid band of bid consultants are attached firmly to the Olympic ship, offering expertise and knowledge transfers while also securing significant fees. The IOC now vets this consultant class and manages a 'Register of Consultants'.[54]

In 1962, the IOC created an International Olympic Aid Committee that, in 1981, became the Olympic Solidarity Commission. The Commission doles out athlete scholarships as well as technical assistance to prospective Olympians in need. The 2016 Rio Olympics marked the inauguration of the Refugee Olympic Team, devised to identify and support refugee athletes with aspirations to participate in the Olympics and other international competitions. The Olympic Solidarity Commission also oversees an Athlete Career Transition programme meant to help Olympians adjust to life after sport.[55]

The IOC provides financial support to OCOGs: for the postponed Tokyo Games, it gave $1.89 billion to the Tokyo Organizing Committee. The IOC also hands out funds to each of the 206 NOCs, IFs overseeing Olympic sports, and groups like WADA, the International Testing Agency (which helps with anti-doping efforts), the International Paralympic Committee,[56] and the International Council of Arbitration of Sport (which works astride CAS).[57] One analysis by German investigative journalist Jens Weinreich found that of the 28 IFs for sports in the Summer Olympics, 15 are fully dependent on IOC funding for their existence. This structural reliance on the IOC, he argues, sets the stage for subservience; largesse can also be a form of control.[58]

Olympic athletes are increasingly noting that for a non-profit organization, the IOC is tremendously profitable. Meanwhile, many Olympians struggle financially. To be sure, not all Olympic athletes are created equal: there's a gaping chasm between fiscally insulated professional players and athletes from lesser-known sports for whom the Games are their one big moneymaking opportunity. Ahead of the Rio 2016 Olympics, more than 100 US athletes started GoFundMe pages to support their Olympic dreams.[59] Research from the athlete-led group Global Athlete and Toronto Metropolitan University found that Olympians receive only 4.1 per cent of Olympic revenues – and only 0.5 per cent directly – compared to professional leagues like the National Basketball Association, the National Football League, the National Hockey League, Major League Baseball, and the English Premier League of football where athletes receive between 45 and 60 per cent of revenues.[60] Independent Athlete groups like the Athletics Association and the International Swimmers' Alliance have formed to fight for athlete rights inside the Olympic system. Athlete advocacy – as well as athlete activism – features in Olympic history, a topic we turn to next.

2
A BRIEF POLITICAL HISTORY OF THE OLYMPICS

When it came to the Olympics, Baron Pierre de Coubertin was an unwavering enthusiast to the very end. Ambition rippled through him. In the face of doubters, he thundered forward with his Olympic vision. Coubertin had a knack for creating potent Olympic symbology, whether it was the iconic five-ring logo, which he devised in 1913, or the Olympic motto – *Citius, Altius, Fortius* (Faster, Higher, Stronger) – which he borrowed in 1894 from the Dominican priest Henri Didon.[1] His flair for theatricality even extended through his death: Coubertin left instructions in his will to carve his heart from his corpse and entomb it in Olympia, Greece. On 26 March 1938, his heart was buried in a marble urn, just metres from the ancient Olympic stadium.[2]

Coubertin was fascinated by the ancient Olympics in Greece, which took place in Olympia from 776 BCE through 261 CE, and he strategically linked the Panhellenic Games of antiquity to his *fin de siècle* Olympic project. The Baron explained that '[t]he Olympic games, with the ancients, controlled athletics and promoted peace. It is not visionary to look to them for similar benefactions in the future'.[3] He diligently worked his international connections – mostly in Western Europe – to build support for his Olympic project. In 1894 he convened his carefully selected allies in Paris – including the King of Belgium, the Prince of Wales, and the Crown Prince of Greece – where they hammered out a plan to stage the first modern Games in Athens two years later.[4]

From the beginning, the modern Olympics tip-toed the tightrope between fostering internationalism and instigating chauvinism. Coubertin believed that the Olympics could be 'a potent, if indirect, factor in securing universal peace'.[5] However, he was drawn to the power of sport in part because he viewed it as the means by which the French nation could reinvigorate itself after the humiliation of the 1870–1871 Franco-Prussian War. He famously proclaimed, 'I shall burnish a flabby and cramped youth, its body and its character, by sport, its risks and even its excesses'.[6] He viewed sport as 'a marvelous instrument for "virilization"'.[7] Towards the end of his life, in 1935, he stated that Olympism:

> is an *aristocracy*, an *elite*. Of course the aristocracy is completely egalitarian in origin since its membership is determined solely by the physical superiority of the

individual, by his muscular ability. ... Not all young men are destined to become athletes. Later, no doubt, through enhanced public and private hygiene and through astute measures intended to improve the race, it will be possible greatly to increase the number of individuals capable of handling intense athletic education.[8]

The Baron's cosmopolitan internationalism was forever in tension with his passionate nationalism, and he embedded this contradiction at the heart of the Olympics.

The Olympics have come a long way since the zealous French aristocrat chiselled the Games from Greek antiquity. But even in the Baron's time, behind the shimmering scrim of Olympism, controversies and contradictions lurked. Until his dying day, Coubertin doggedly clutched a basket of isms – classism, racism, and sexism – and these tendencies cannot be brushed off by suggesting he was simply a man of his times. The Baron's biases became ingrained in the Games, affecting how they were organized from the outset.

The Baron was, after all, a baron. His family tree was chock-full of nobility on both sides. Reared by nobles, Coubertin signed his epistles with his title throughout his life. Aristocrats of the era were trained to embrace vocations, not professions. Coubertin's biographer notes that the aristocratic ethos exalting amateur status encouraged the Baron, as an *homme de noblesse*, to 'act disinterestedly for the love of Faith, the Motherland, Nature, Art, Humanity'.[9]

In the early days of the Games, Coubertin and his associates adopted a definition of amateurism from

19th-century Victorian England that disqualified waged workers whether or not their jobs were linked to sport. The Amateur Athletic Club in England assigned professional status to anyone who worked as a 'mechanic, artisan, or labourer'. Working-class labourers were denied amateur status, thereby opening wide the sports fields for 'gentlemen amateurs' to excel. Although this rule was adjusted in England in the 1880s, '[r]ules against any profit replaced the rule against the working class', notes scholar David Young. 'The effect was nearly the same.'[10]

The amateur code was bricked into Olympic ideology, allowing the International Olympic Committee (IOC) to regulate the participation of working people. The strict definition of Olympic amateurism had to be revised in the early 1900s, mostly because of the popularity of professional soccer in England.[11] And yet, Coubertin himself benefited from the leeway given to 'gentlemen amateurs'. At the 1912 Olympics in Stockholm, the literary jury awarded the gold medal in literature to Coubertin for his poem 'Ode to Sport'. To dupe jurists, he submitted his entry under two pseudonyms, Georges Hohrod and M. Eschbach, although scholars believe the art jury knew exactly who was getting the gold.[12]

Coubertin also held racist views. He upbraided 'the natural indolence of the Oriental'[13] and argued that 'the theory proposing that all human races have equal rights leads to a line of policy which hinders any progress in the colonies'. He believed 'the superior race is fully entitled to deny the lower race certain privileges of civilized life'.[14] Coubertin was open to include African nations in the Olympics because he thought the Games could ameliorate Africans' supposed inferiority. In 1923, he asserted:

> It may appear premature to introduce the principle of sports competitions into a continent that is behind the times and among peoples still without elementary culture – and particularly presumptuous to expect this expansion to lead to a speeding up of the march of civilization in these countries. Let us think, however, for a moment, of what is troubling the African soul. Untapped forces – individual laziness and a sort of collective need for action – a thousand resentments, and a thousand jealousies of the white man and yet, at the same time, the wish to imitate him and thus share his privileges.[15]

He then opined that sport might be of service to Africans since it 'helps create order and clarify thought', so steps should be taken to assist Africa in joining the Olympic Movement.[16]

As mentioned in Chapter 1, Coubertin believed the Olympics should be the domain of men alone. He viewed women as 'the weaker sex'[17] and stated that their participation in sport was 'impractical, uninteresting, ungainly, and, I do not hesitate to add, improper'.[18] For the Baron, a 'woman's glory rightfully came through the number and quality of children she produced, and … where sports were concerned, her greatest accomplishment was to encourage her sons to excel rather than to seek records for herself'.[19] He argued for 'the solemn and periodic exaltation of male athleticism ... with the applause of women as a reward'.[20] His sexist views on women and sport did not evolve. In 1934 – three years before he died of a heart attack at age 74 – Coubertin stated, 'I continue to think that association with women's athleticism is bad ... and that such athleticism should be excluded from the Olympic programme'.[21]

Against Coubertin's wishes – and contrary to medical theories at the time that asserted women bike riders could get a strange malady called 'bicycle face', replete with permanently bulging eyeballs and a tightened jaw – women did participate in the early days of the Games.[22] Although they were excluded from competing at the first modern Games, held in Athens in 1896, 22 women took part in the Paris 1900 Olympics in tennis and golf. Four years later, six women participated at the 1904 Games in St. Louis, before rising to 38 competitors at the 1908 London Olympics.[23]

Let the Games begin!

The first modern Olympics nearly didn't happen. After Coubertin and his allies decided in 1894 to revive the Games, they had only two years to prepare, and the Greek government decidedly lacked enthusiasm. Coubertin vowed the Games would not bankrupt Greece, but locals were suspicious. When IOC President Demetrios Vikelas told the Prime Minister of Greece about the event, the latter 'would have very much preferred that the question of the Olympic

Games had never arisen'.[24] But Coubertin's aristocratic allies in Greece stepped up to help. King George and Crown Prince Constantine convinced Greek business tycoon George Averoff to fund stadium construction in Athens. Averoff offered a million drachmas, which saved the day but also threw into question Coubertin's assertion that the entire Olympic budget would be 'in the neighborhood of 250,000 Drachmas'.[25] Lowballing Olympic costs would become a notable – and controversial – trend.

Trade unions and working people across Athens rallied to the Olympic cause, which was ironic since the 'mechanics clause' made them ineligible to participate.[26] Sport historian David Goldblatt dubbed Olympic athletes at the inaugural Games 'part of a transnational class of bourgeois athletes'. Italian Carlo Airoldi, a working-class long-distance runner, funded his journey to Athens by running there, with monetary support from an Italian newspaper and winnings from recent races. Upon his arrival in Athens, he was denied amateur status and thus the right to participate.[27]

The 1896 Olympics were enormously popular in Athens. The Games' opening ceremony was the largest peaceful gathering of humanity since antiquity, with 50,000 people filling Averoff's stadium and another 20,000 observing from the nearby hillside. Two hundred and forty-five athletes from 14 countries participated in nine sports, with the biggest contingent – 81 competitors – from Greece. Greek spectators cheered on local farmer Spyridon Louis in the marathon, and he obliged them with victory. Averoff reportedly pledged that the marathon champion could marry his daughter, but Louis was already betrothed.[28] Four decades later, during the opening ceremony of the 1936 Berlin Olympics, Louis would offer a literal olive branch to Adolf Hitler.[29]

Intoxicated by success, King George of Greece decreed at the end of the Games that Greeks would host all future Olympic competitions, making Athens 'the tranquil and permanent seat of the Olympic Games'.[30] Coubertin was aghast, viewing the King's declaration as 'a rash, thoughtless step'.[31] The 1900 Olympics were already scheduled for Paris, after all. Coubertin gently noted that the IOC 'agreed that every country should celebrate the Olympic games in turn'.[32] After the Athens 1896 Olympics, Vikelas resigned as IOC president and Coubertin took the helm. He held the presidency until 1925, when the 62-year-old retired.

To the chagrin of the Baron, the next three Olympics – Paris 1900, St. Louis 1904, and London 1908 – were attached to the World's Fair, gigantic extravaganzas known for entertainment, cuisine, and popular culture. Although this was not exactly what Coubertin desired – he called it an 'unholy union' – it allowed the Games to inch forward.[33] The Olympics were essentially relegated to being a sporty sideshow alongside international expositions that stretched on for months. The 1900 Exposition Universelle in Paris lasted five months and organizers blended sport competitions into other events, confusing some athletes, who returned home unsure that they had actually participated in the

Olympics. French marathoner Michel Théato won his race in two hours and 59 minutes, but he only had his victory as an Olympic champion confirmed more than a decade later.[34]

The 1904 St. Louis Games convened 687 athletes, with a whopping 525 from the host country and another 41 from Canada. The US took 80 of 99 gold medals and 242 of 279 medals overall, although tracking medal winners, distances, and times was unreliable at best. Once again, the World's Fair spread across months, from May through November.[35] The Games were stained by the inclusion of a series of athletic events that pitted ethnic and racial groups against each other, thereby allowing social scientists and sport power brokers to test their racist hypotheses. These 'Anthropology Days', which were often called the 'Special Olympics', were a brazen exercise in White supremacy that organizers dubbed 'the first athletic meeting held anywhere, in which savages were exclusive participants'.[36] Although the Anthropology Days were not an official Olympic event, they were used to drum up support for the Games that followed. Anthropologist Nancy Parezo sums up the affair as 'a comedy in bad science' in the service of a racist strain of social Darwinism.[37] Coubertin, who chose not to attend the St. Louis Olympics, called Anthropology Days 'a mistake' and 'inhuman'.[38] The official history of the Olympics conceded that '[f]or the third time, a modern Olympic Games was a near disaster'.[39]

Although Coubertin successfully rebuffed King George's attempt to permanently seat the Games in Athens, the zealous Greeks were allowed to stage interim Olympics in 1906. The IOC does not include these Games in its official records – and Coubertin once again declined to attend, opting instead to join an 'Olympic Arts Exhibition' in Paris – but it approved naming the event the 'Athens International Olympic Games'.[40]

The 1906 intercalary Games were marked by an extraordinary act of athlete activism, a bright thread running through the Olympics' historical tapestry. Enter Peter O'Connor, an accomplished track athlete from Ireland who, along with three fellow countrymen – Con Leahy, John Daly, and John McGough – was forced to participate for Great Britain because Ireland was ruled from Westminster at the time and did not have its own National Olympic Committee.[41] O'Connor – a working-class clerk and an ardent Irish nationalist – was incensed.[42] At the 'March of Nations' before the Games, the Irish athletes donned green blazers emblazoned with golden shamrocks on the left breast along with matching green caps similarly adorned (see Figure 2.1). The athletes hung back behind the rest of the British contingent, conspicuously distancing themselves.[43] O'Connor's granddaughter, Rosemarie O'Connor Quinn, said: 'He was a fiery man. He was not a man to be crossing.'[44]

After winning silver in the long jump, O'Connor executed an epic act of political dissent. During the medal ceremonies, he sprinted over to the flagpole where the Union Jack was hoisted high and shimmied up it, unfurling a large green flag bearing a golden

Figure 2.1: Irish track athlete Peter O'Connor

Peter O'Connor was forced to compete for Great Britain at the 1906 Olympics in Athens. In protest, he wore a green blazer emblazoned with a golden shamrock. He also climbed a flag pole in protest, waving a banner that read 'Erin go Bragh' or 'Ireland Forever'.

harp and the words 'Erin Go Bragh' ('Ireland Forever'). Below, his teammate Con Leahy waved a similar flag and fended off the Greek police, giving O'Connor additional time atop the pole.[45] O'Connor's great grandson, Mark Quinn, later wrote that '[t]he Irishman's points might well be accredited to Great Britain, but the flying of the Irish flag left none in doubt as to where O'Connor's true allegiances lay'.[46] Athlete activism would become an Olympic tradition of sorts, if one condemned by the IOC.

The 1908 Olympics in London – attached to the Franco-British Exposition – brought together more than 2,000 athletes from 22 countries. Great Britain made the biggest medal haul, winning 56 golds and 146 medals altogether.[47] The country imprinted its stamp on sport in other ways, too. In response to monarchical whims, the marathon started on the lawns of Windsor Castle. King Edward and Queen Alexandra wanted their grandchildren to witness the beginning of the race without having to depart their property. This decision meant the distance of the marathon was 26 miles, 385 yards – same as today.[48]

Politics bubbled up when the hosts forgot to include the US and Swedish flags at the opening ceremony.[49] The US, in turn, ignited a political firestorm when its flag bearer refused to dip the stars and stripes in deference to the British monarchy during the opening ceremony.[50] Ahead of the Games, the *New York Times* decried Olympic amateurism's class bias, pointing to the 'American oarsmen' who 'have been discriminated against' by the Amateur Rowing Association of Great Britain's definition of amateurism. The newspaper noted, 'no artisan, laborer, or mechanic or man who does manual work for a living may compete', which was 'a direct slap at American amateurs, most of whom are of the working class'.[51] Meanwhile, feminist activists like Emmeline Pankhurst used the Games as a springboard for suffrage, promising to disrupt the proceedings if organizers excluded women athletes. To protest, suffragettes shovelled up golf courses and left messages like 'No Votes, No Golf'.[52]

But the Olympics found their groove four years later in Stockholm where the Games were organized independently from the international expositions and received avid support from their Swedish hosts, including Olympic super-fan King Gustav V. Much enthusiasm revolved around US athlete Jim Thorpe, a Native American of Sac and Fox and Potawatomi descent who won both the pentathlon and the decathlon.[53] Thorpe's Native name was Wa-Tho-Huk – 'Bright Path' – and he was unequivocally the brightest star of the Games; the Olympics provided a platform for Indigenous excellence to shine. After the Olympics, though, news emerged that Thorpe had previously received around $60 per month for playing semiprofessional baseball. The IOC stripped him of his medals, making him a high-profile victim of the amateur code.[54] It wasn't until 1982 that the IOC returned his gold medals, presenting his children with replacements the following year.[55] In 2022, the IOC rewrote the record books and officially reinstated Thorpe as the sole gold-medal-winner for both events.[56]

After the Thorpe controversy, Coubertin authored an Olympic oath to reinforce the importance of amateurism. It read: 'We swear that we are taking part in the Olympic Games as loyal competitors, observing the rules governing the Games, and anxious to show a spirit of chivalry for the honour of our countries and for the glory of sport.'[57] Coubertin wrote, '[b]eside its wonderful moral value, the athlete's oath is proving to be the only practical means to put an end to this intolerable state of affairs', which, he clarified, meant 'disguised professionalism'.[58] The oath was first implemented at the 1920 Antwerp Olympics because the First World War made the 1916 Olympics – planned for Berlin – untenable.[59] The Olympic flag also debuted in Antwerp, after making its first public appearance in 1914 at the twentieth anniversary of the IOC. In April 1915, amid the war, the IOC moved its headquarters from Paris to neutral Switzerland, sinking roots in Lausanne.[60]

After the First World War, the Olympics re-emerged in Antwerp, a politically symbolic choice, as Belgium had endured a vicious German invasion. Political nationalism rippled through Europe, and only intensified when Games organizers opted not to invite Germany, Austria, Bulgaria, Hungary, and Turkey. Coubertin objected, but the IOC quietly tolerated the snub.[61] Germany did not reappear at the Olympics until 1928, after the 1924 Games, which returned to Paris as a way to honour Coubertin's indefatigable dedication to the Games. The Olympiad included the first-ever Winter Olympics in Chamonix, France a few months before the Summer Games in Paris.[62]

Meanwhile, women's participation at the Olympics essentially flatlined. Sixty-three women participated in Antwerp, but this was a tiny uptick: between 1900 and 1920, the percentage of Olympic participants who were women increased from 2.2 per cent to 2.4 per cent.[63] But gumption and ingenuity emerged from exclusion. In the 1920s and 1930s, women and their allies organized alternative games called the Women's Olympics. In total they staged four competitions – in 1922, 1926, 1930, and 1934 – with participants from around the world, if mostly from North America, Western Europe, and Japan. The IOC's response foreshadowed its intense brand protection: it compelled a name change to the 'Women's World Games' to avoid referencing the 'Olympics'.[64]

More than 20,000 people attended the inaugural 1922 Women's Olympics in Paris. Athletes from five countries – Britain, Czechoslovakia, France, Switzerland, and the US – competed in 11 events. The next installation, four years later in Gothenburg, featured athletes from eight countries. In 1930, Prague hosted a three-day event with more than 200 elite athletes from 17 countries. The fourth and final Women's Olympics were held in London in 1934, with 19 participating countries.[65] The events drew sizable crowds and pulverized the fiction that women were too fragile for sport. The success of these alternative events placed pressure on Olympic brass to integrate women into the Games in greater numbers.

Working-class activists produced their own alternative to what they called the 'bourgeois Olympics'. They organized Workers' Olympics with an ethos that merged sport, international socialism, and working-class solidarity. Organizers viewed sports not as an opiate of the masses, but a lever for political consciousness-raising. The Workers' Games were more about health than competition, and people from all races, ethnicities, and genders were welcome to take part. Organized primarily by European socialists, these Games took place in Frankfurt (1925), Vienna (1931), and Antwerp (1937). The rise of fascist Francisco Franco in Spain derailed the Olimpiada Popular de Barcelona planned for 1936, and then the Second World War put a damper on the entire endeavour, sabotaging another Workers' Games planned for 1943 in Helsinki.[66]

The Workers' Olympics were major events. The inaugural installation in Frankfurt included 150,000 participants from 19 countries. In Vienna, 80,000 worker-athletes from 23 countries participated.[67] Around 250,000 people watched the finale, a 'festive march' featuring approximately 100,000 athletes.[68] Vienna's socialist government constructed a sparkling $1 million stadium.[69] In 1937, around 27,000 worker-athletes from 17 countries competed in Antwerp and 200,000 people joined the final march through the city.[70]

Olympic politicization intensifies

If the 1920 Olympics in Antwerp conjured political glimmers, the Berlin 1936 Olympics – also known as the Nazi Games – cast a gargantuan political spotlight. German Propaganda Minister Joseph Goebbels was enthusiastic about the Olympics, viewing them as a chance to spread the Nazis' White-supremacist messaging far and wide.[71] To facilitate this, organizers invented the Olympic Torch Relay for the 1936 Games, a tradition that has continued through today. A flame lit at Mount Olympus in Greece zigzagged its way to Berlin's newly built stadium, where it ignited the Olympic cauldron. The torch relay – approved by the IOC in 1934 – featured more than 3,000 runners and passed through numerous countries that Hitler, a few years later, invaded and occupied. The event rhymed with Nazi propaganda asserting German Aryans as the true heirs of the ancient Greeks.[72]

Politics were everywhere at the Games' opening ceremony. Athletes marched in by country, per Olympic custom, thereby stoking political nationalism. Due to marked similarities between the Olympic salute and the Nazi 'Heil' – the extended arm of the Olympic gesture was angled a bit to the side, with an open hand and palm down, whereas the 'Heil' salute ramrodded straight ahead – political confusion reigned. When Canadian and French Olympians gave the Olympic salute, the crowd interpreted it as a Nazi 'Heil', detonating applause.[73] Meanwhile, Bulgarian athletes jabbed skyward an enthusiastic Nazi salute while goose-stepping. Italian athletes gave the fascist salute in Hitler's direction. The German Olympic team carried an enormous Nazi banner.[74] The 1936 Olympics in Berlin are an early example of 'sportswashing': when political leaders use sports to appear legitimate on the global stage, exploiting mega-events to try to launder their stained reputations, ramp up nationalism, and distract domestic publics from chronic problems.[75]

The aged Coubertin was unable to travel to Berlin for the Games, but his memorable words projected from the stadium loudspeakers: 'The important thing in the Olympic Games is not winning but taking part; the essential thing in life is not conquering but fighting well.'[76] After the Games, he concluded, '[t]he wonderful success of the Berlin Games has served the Olympic ideal magnificently'.[77] But behind the scenes, the Nazis had secured the Baron's support by promising to nominate him for the Nobel Peace Prize. More perniciously, after Coubertin had fallen on hard financial times, the Nazis essentially bribed him, offering him 10,000 Reichsmarks, a sum worth hundreds of thousands of dollars today. The funds were meant to venerate the Baron's key historical role in reviving the Games, at least in theory. In practice, however, the money had the effect of silencing him, as he could not publicly admit that he had accepted such a colossal sum.[78]

Black athletes from the US were eminently successful in Berlin, not only smashing records but also the Nazis' racist theories. Jesse Owens, the African American track sensation, won gold medals in the 100-metre race, the 200-metre run, the long jump, and the 400-metre relay team, setting world and Olympic records along the way.[79] Eighteen Black athletes represented the US in Berlin, 12 in track and field, four in boxing, and two in weightlifting. US Black track athletes hauled in six gold medals and secured 83 of their country's 167 points. Hitler's Aryan-supremacy ideology took a public beating on the world's biggest sporting stage.[80]

In the wake of the Second World War – which forced the cancellation of the 1940 and 1944 Olympics – the Games became a political crucible, a sporty Cold War proxy battlefield of sorts. Joseph Stalin recognized the magnitude of international sport – one of his guiding slogans was 'We won the war, we should win in sport!' – and with his blessing, Soviet athletes embraced international competition with more verve, beginning

Figure 2.2: Jesse Owens

Jesse Owens participating
in the 200-metre final at the
1936 Berlin Olympics. He
won the gold medal.

in 1945, replete with financial support from the state. By 1951, the USSR's Konstantin Andrianov was co-opted as an IOC member and Soviet athletes were busily preparing for the 1952 Olympics in Helsinki.[81]

The emergence of the Soviet Union as a sporting powerhouse not only stoked nationalistic intrigue, but also improved the quality of Olympic competition. In Helsinki, Olympic records were set in every women's track and field event except the high jump. In men's track and field, 21 Olympic records and three world records were eclipsed.[82] Globally, journalists covering the Games paid ever more attention to the Olympic medal counts. The Soviets won 100 medals, including 29 golds, while Hungary hauled in 16 gold medals and 42 overall. Czech runner Emil Zátopek triumphed in the marathon as well as the 5,000-metre and 10,000-metre races.[83] Different ways of tabulating points yielded different victors, a dynamic captured in one *New York Times* headline: 'Russians Hail Olympic "Victory" But Fail to Substantiate Claim: Pravda Cites "World Superiority" of Soviet Athletes in Helsinki Games Without Providing Tabulation of Points.'[84]

Once again, sport emerged as politics by other means. Fierce rivalries between the Eastern and Western blocs often overshadowed goodwill in Helsinki – opposing blocs even stayed in separate Olympic villages. The USSR erected a gigantic portrait of Stalin outside its base camp as well as smaller likenesses of leaders of Soviet satellites like Czechoslovakia, Hungary, and Poland. The USSR was well-known for financially supporting its athletes so they could train full time, raising questions about their amateur status. Doping allegations also bobbed to the surface after the Soviet Union's weightlifting team exceeded expectations in Helsinki. Performance-enhancing drugs were becoming a bigger issue in general, especially after numerous speed skaters at the 1952 Winter Games in Oslo were sickened from consuming amphetamine stimulants.[85]

Then there was the prickly 'two-China problem': the battle between the People's Republic of China (PRC) and Taiwan that spilled into the sports world when both bodies pursued the IOC's recognition. In 1949, as Chinese Communists under Mao Zedong ascended to power, Nationalists led by Chiang Kai-shek fled to Taipei. (Taiwan – or the Republic of China – held a seat at the UN until 1971 when it was replaced by the PRC.) This set up a diplomatic quandary that would dog the IOC – and the wider world – for decades, with both

Beijing and Taipei aggressively pressing for the other's exclusion from the Games. The IOC didn't help when it inadvertently issued invitations to the 1952 Helsinki Olympics to both Communists and Nationalists on the day before the Games began. Although the PRC's Olympic delegation arrived in Finland only a day before the closing ceremony – so only one athlete, a swimmer, competed – mainland China participated in cultural programming and its flag flew alongside other participating countries.[86]

As an IOC vice president, Avery Brundage had a front-row seat to the unfolding drama. Brundage grew up working class in Chicago before becoming a construction-industry tycoon. He played a decisive role in stanching calls in the US to boycott the 1936 Berlin Games over the Nazis' anti-Semitism and racism. Before that, he competed at the 1912 Olympics against Jim Thorpe. At the IOC session accompanying the 1952 Helsinki Olympics, Brundage ascended to the presidency of the IOC, defeating Lord David Burghley of Britain.[87]

The Official History of the Olympic Games and the IOC describes Brundage as 'despotic', 'a moral bulldozer', and a 'fanatical defender of de Coubertin's legacy'.[88] He shared Coubertin's opinion that the Olympics and politics should not mix. 'We actively combat the introduction of politics into the Olympic movement', he wrote, 'and are adamant against the use of the Olympic Games as a tool or as a weapon by any organization'.[89] When it came to amateurism, Brundage and Coubertin sang from the same hymnal.

Brundage asserted that athlete commercialism 'could be considered a violation of the rights of man'.[90] He pushed to 'keep the Games clean, pure and honest, and free from politics and dollar signs'.[91]

Brundage was staunchly conservative, and this came through unambiguously in his personal notes. 'Social security and other socialist measures gives [sic] support to the lazy, the worthless, and the shiftless', he wrote. 'Society thus destroys itself by interferring [sic] with nature's laws, which eliminates those who are unwilling to take care of themselves. It is the same with medication, which extends the life of the unhealthy and eventually destroys virile society.'[92] To him, '[t]he whole philosophy of Social Security is wrong'. He adopted the extreme view that '[o]ur system will never be a success unless those who have no responsibilities are not permitted to vote'. He also opined that '[w]e take care of the lazy and shiftless instead of forcing them to work'.[93] Autocrats were just fine by him. 'An intelligent, beneficent dictatorship is the most efficient form of government', he wrote. 'Observe what happened in Germany for six or seven years in the 1930's.'[94] When it came to the IOC, a conservative organization chock-full of aristocrats, Brundage's views were not outside the mainstream.

Anti-racism and the Games

The Olympic Movement was unable to sidestep the racial politics of the 1960s and 1970s. Until then, despite its racist apartheid policies, South Africa remained welcome in the Olympic family. The IOC trusted South African sports officials when they said they did not exclude athletes from their Olympic squads based on race, despite evidence to the contrary. Brundage wanted to keep South Africa inside the Olympic fold, but his colleagues disagreed, and they voted to withdraw the country's invitation to the 1964 Tokyo Games.[95] South Africa's exclusion continued at the 1968 Olympics in Mexico City, after 39 nations promised to boycott the Games if the country was readmitted.[96] In 1970, the IOC officially expelled South Africa from the Olympic Movement. The country didn't participate again until 1992, by which time the apartheid regime was finally being dismantled.

South Africa's exclusion was supported in the US by a collection of elite athletes called the Olympic Project for Human Rights (OPHR), who were advocating for racial justice and international solidarity. Among the OPHR's demands was the 'Curtailment of participation of all-white teams and individuals from the Union of South Africa and Southern Rhodesia in all United States Olympic Athletic events'. The group also pushed for the 'Restoration of Muhammad Ali's title' and the 'Removal of the anti-semitic and anti-black personality Avery Brundage from his post as Chairman of the International Olympic Committee.'[97]

The OPHR considered boycotting the 1968 Mexico City Olympics, but instead decided to attend and encourage its athletes to promote justice. US track stars Tommie Smith and John Carlos did just that, creating an iconic moment. After winning gold and bronze in the 200-metre dash, they stood atop the medal stand and protested pervasive poverty and racism in the US and the wider world by punching their black-glove-clad fists skyward as they bowed their heads during the national anthem. Their shoeless feet and black socks symbolized poverty. The gloves signified Black pride. Carlos wore his jacket open to represent his family's working-class roots. Both men attached OPHR buttons onto their track jackets. Australian Peter Norman, who won silver, wore a button in solidarity.[98]

Brundage was irate. He pressured the US Olympic Committee to suspend Carlos and Smith from the team and dismiss them from the Olympic Village. The Committee obliged, releasing a statement that slammed the athletes for their 'untypical exhibitionism' that 'violates the basic standards of sportsmanship and good manners'. The group then threatened that '[a] repetition of such incidents by other members of the US team can only be considered a willful disregard of Olympic principles that would warrant the severest penalties'.[99]

Two days prior to Carlos and Smith's indelible act of dissent, US Olympic sprinter Wyomia Tyus, the first Olympian to win back-to-back gold in the 100-metre dash, had also taken a subtle stand for justice: 'As part of my contribution to the protest for human rights, I had worn black running shorts', she said, 'rather than the regular white running shorts that were issued to us'. After winning gold in the 4×100 relay, journalists asked her what she thought of Carlos and Smith's protest. She recalled stating, 'We all know that we're fighting for human rights. That's what they stood for on the victory stand – human rights for everyone, everywhere. And to support that and to support them, I'm dedicating my medal to them. I believe in what they did.'[100] Tyus was not the only women athlete speaking out for justice at the 1968 Mexico City Games. As mentioned in Chapter 1, Czech gymnast Věra Čáslavská dissented against imperialism, dipping her head in silent protest during the Russian national anthem.

The spirit of dissent continued at the 1972 Munich Olympics. After winning gold and silver in the 400-metre run, US Olympic sprinters Vincent Matthews and Wayne Collett shared the top tier of the medal stand – typically reserved for the gold-medal-winner alone – an act of unity that broke Olympic protocol. During the US national anthem, they angled their backs away from the flag and stood casually, projecting disinterest (see Figure 2.3). Matthews rubbed his chin pensively before folding his arms in front of himself. Collett stood barefoot, track jacket open, with hands on hips. As the African American athletes departed the ceremony, Matthews twirled his medal on his finger while Collett thrust a clenched fist into the air.[101] 'For me, not standing at attention meant that I wasn't going along with a program dictated by ... those John Wayne types – my Country right or wrong', Matthews wrote in his memoir.[102] Collett stated, 'I couldn't stand there and sing the words because I don't believe they're true. I wish they were. I think we have the potential to have a beautiful country, but I don't think we do'.[103] Not only were the athletes kicked out of the Munich

Figure 2.3: US track athletes Vincent Matthews and Wayne Collett

Vincent Matthews and Wayne Collett stand casually atop the podium after winning gold and silver medals in the 400-metre run at the 1972 Munich Games. In response, the IOC issued a lifetime ban for both athletes; it was eventually rescinded in 2022.

Olympics, but they also received lifetime bans from the IOC.[104] Afterwards, the IOC adapted the Olympic Charter to read: 'Every kind of demonstration or propaganda, whether political, religious or racial, in the Olympic areas is forbidden.'[105] More than 50 years after the medal-stand action, the IOC finally rescinded its ban.[106]

The Munich Olympics were marred when members of a Palestinian group called Black September snuck into the Olympic Village and kidnapped 11 Israeli athletes. This eventually led to a gun battle with the German authorities in which all the Israeli athletes and five Palestinians were killed on the airport tarmac as they prepared to board a plane. In the wake of the terrorist attack, Brundage insisted that 'The Games must go on'. After a one-day hiatus, they did.[107]

The Olympics pivot ... and commercialize

The year 1976 marked a momentous pivot for the Olympics: activists in Denver forced the relocation of the 1976 Winter Games to Innsbruck, while the Montreal Summer Olympics went far over budget, plunging the city into debt.

In May 1970, the IOC selected Denver to host the 1976 Winter Olympics. After winning the bid battle, Colorado Governor John Love promised the Games would benefit all Coloradans. A coalition of environmental activists and fiscal conservatives disagreed, organizing a campaign against the Olympics. Organizations like the Rocky Mountain Center on Environment and Citizens for Colorado's Future rallied local residents and implored IOC officials to relocate the Games. Crucially, they placed a state bond referendum on the ballot where voters overwhelmingly rejected funding the Olympics.[108] This forced the IOC to relocate the Games to Innsbruck, making Denver the first and only city to spurn the Olympics after being chosen to host. The imbroglio showed the Games could be a site of political fightback.

Meanwhile, Montreal was preparing to host the 1976 Summer Games. In 1973, the head of its organizing committee vowed that the Games would be 'self-financing, without adding in any way to the Canadian taxpayers' burden, without any special subsidy of any type whatsoever', aside from national lottery funds and a federal programme for commemorative coins and postage stamps.[109] Jean Drapeau, the charismatic mayor of Montreal, infamously claimed that '[t]he Montreal Olympics can no more have a deficit, than a man can have a baby'.[110] However, in the end, the Games cost $1.5 billion. The debt wasn't repaid until 2006.[111] Taken together, machinations in Denver and Montreal sent a piercing message to the IOC: they needed to conjure a sustainable funding model. This facilitated the full-throttle commercialization of the Olympics.

Enter business magnate Peter Ueberroth and the 1984 Los Angeles Olympics. Only two cities bid on the 1984 Games – LA and Tehran – and the latter withdrew because of Iran's emergent revolution. This gave LA unprecedented leverage and Mayor Tom Bradley used it, refusing to sign the standard host-city contract that made the host responsible for cost overruns. Also, in light of the Montreal debacle, Los Angeles amended its charter to prohibit financing the Games with public money, restricting taxpayer funding to a $5 million hotel tax and an Olympic ticket tax.[112] The LA bid team essentially privatized the effort, installing Ueberroth to orchestrate fundraising and Games organizing. He convinced the US Olympic Committee to share financial responsibility for the Games alongside LA organizers. The IOC grudgingly agreed, disregarding a rule in its own charter prohibiting such activity.[113]

Ueberroth, an evangelist of capitalism, saw the Games as 'a powerful instrument to demonstrate the validity of the American free enterprise system'.[114] To construct the Olympic swimming pool and velodrome and refurbish the LA Coliseum, he brought on corporate partners like Atlantic Richfield Company and McDonald's. He brokered a television deal with ABC for a record-breaking $225 million.[115] Ueberroth recruited an exclusive club of corporate sponsors that supplied a minimum of $4 million in cash or in-kind goods, as mentioned in Chapter 1. In addition to the 35 companies that joined the programme – such as American Express, Anheuser-Busch, AT&T, Atari, General Motors, Converse, Mars, Motorola, Westinghouse, and Xerox – 'official suppliers' included Adidas, Panasonic, Rawlings Sporting Goods, and Toshiba.[116] Sociologist Alan Tomlinson marked the moment as the 'Disneyfication' of the Olympics.[117]

The 1984 Games were a fiscal win, generating a surplus of around $215 million, although this does not account for significant public subsidies that buoyed the Games, such as taxpayer-funded communication networks, busing services, and policing. In addition, the federal government largely covered security outlays and, in line with Olympic custom, thousands of volunteers reduced labour costs.[118]

Ahead of the Games, McDonald's publicized a nationwide promotion promising free food and drinks every time a US athlete medalled. After the Soviet Union and many of its allies boycotted the Games – in response to the US boycott of the 1980 Olympics in Moscow over the Soviet invasion of Afghanistan – US athletes went on to win a whopping 174 medals, 83 of them gold, including four won by track star Carl Lewis, spurring a shortage of Big Macs in some US cities.[119] Moroccan 400-metre hurdler Nawal El Moutawakel won her country's first Olympic gold in LA; she went on to become a member of the IOC in 1998.[120]

The fact that Los Angeles did not haemorrhage money like Montreal, and even scored a surplus, helped steady the Olympic ship. So too did Juan Antonio Samaranch, the Spaniard who in 1980 became the seventh president of the IOC. Historian David Goldblatt notes that Samaranch had been an unexceptional functionary in Franco's fascist regime and was 'almost entirely bereft of a public persona, virtually inaudible as a public speaker and seemingly disinterested in ideas and intellectual pursuits'. And yet, he notes, Samaranch was a transformational IOC president.[121]

Samaranch embraced and extended the relationship between the Olympics and corporate sponsors while pushing television revenues to ever-greater heights. He helped start 'The Olympic Programme', known today as 'The Olympic Partner Programme'. It launched ahead of the 1988 Seoul Summer Olympics and 1988

Winter Games in Calgary where over the course of the Olympiad (1985–1988) it netted $95 million.[122] For the Olympiad spanning 2017 to 2020–2021, the programme raked in around $2.3 *billion*.[123] In the early 1970s, 98 per cent of the IOC's revenue derived from television rights.[124] The IOC's corporate-sponsor programme lessened this reliance. Today 61 per cent of IOC revenue comes from broadcaster rights.[125]

To be sure, there were some rocky moments under Samaranch's reign. When, in 1981, the IOC selected Seoul to host the 1988 Summer Games, South Korea was ruled by a military dictatorship, and, on the road to the Games, the government displaced more than 700,000 people. Boosters asserted that hosting the Olympics helped smooth the path towards democracy while modernizing the country, but not without tremendous human suffering.[126] The Seoul Games were scarred by scandal when Canadian sprinter Ben Johnson tested positive for the steroid stanozolol as well as probenecid, a banned substance that masks steroids appearing in urine. Although IOC brass framed the positive test as evidence of a successful drug-testing programme, the episode threw into question the integrity of Olympic competition.[127]

Samaranch increased IOC power by deftly enmeshing himself in global sports bodies, cosying up to powerful administrators, and establishing a dense network of contacts in the business world. He amassed power and wielded it with aplomb, taking residence in Lausanne – unlike his predecessor Lord Killanin of Ireland – where he conducted IOC business. Under Samaranch, the IOC voted in 1986 to stagger Summer and Winter Olympics at every two years, starting with the 1994 Winter Games, in order to maximize revenues and keep the Olympics perpetually in the public eye. His biggest triumph may well have been bringing the 1992 Summer Games to Barcelona, an Olympics that some point to as the most successful of the modern era.

The Barcelona Olympics fit puzzle-piece-like into the long-term urban development plan hatched by city leaders a full decade before the IOC granted hosting duties. The Games cost $11.5 billion, with 33 per cent funded by the private sector and 67 per cent from public financing.[128] During the preparation phase, unemployment decreased and the construction industry roared.[129] The city rebuilt the Poblenou industrial area downtown, constructed an Olympic Village that was converted into housing, refurbished the airport, and reduced pollution in the river flowing through the city. Although the Olympics sparked gentrification – reducing the availability of public housing and increasing rents and housing prices – one economist found that the upsides of hosting were 'far more intense and sustained than that of other host cities'.[130] The overall approach became known as the 'Barcelona Model', the aspirational template for future Olympic host cities.

The Games go green

After the groundbreaking 1992 'Earth Summit' in Rio de Janeiro, the United Nations issued 'Agenda 21', its plan for ecologically sustainable development. Olympic power brokers were laying groundwork for a working relationship with the UN, and by 1994, the IOC proclaimed the environment was 'an essential component of Olympism'. In 1995, the IOC amended its Charter, stipulating that 'the Olympic Games are held in conditions which demonstrate a responsible concern for environmental issues'. It inaugurated a Sport and Environment Commission with annual meetings. By 1999, the IOC launched its own 'Agenda 21' that promised to weave environmental sustainability into its overall approach. The IOC delineated sustainability as 'the third pillar of Olympism', alongside sport and culture.[131]

The timing of the IOC's initial interest in sustainability coincided with the first staggered installation of the Winter Olympics: the 1994 Lillehammer Games. Norway's Prime Minister Gro Harlem Brundtland, a prominent conservationist, influenced Games organizers to take environmentalism seriously. Lillehammer organized a 'Compact Games' that limited travel – and thus emissions – while the location of Games venues underwent significant ecological scrutiny, foregrounding forest protection and energy conservation.[132] Norwegian speed skater Johann Olav Koss ignited local fans by winning three gold medals, setting three world records along the way.

A major winner at the Atlanta 1996 Summer Games was Coca-Cola, the Atlanta-based beverage firm and longtime Olympic sponsor (beginning with the 1928 Amsterdam Olympics). Coca-Cola plunged more than

$500 million into sponsorship and marketing, financing the Olympic Torch relay and building a $20-million Coca-Cola theme park in downtown Atlanta.[133] Meanwhile, Atlanta 1996 continued the worrying trend whereby the Games contributed to housing problems in the host city. Rents near the Olympic Park skyrocketed. Public housing was bulldozed to make space for the Olympics, including Techwood Homes, the country's first federally subsidized public housing project, that was displaced by the Olympic Village.[134] In 1995 and 1996 more than 9,000 homeless people were arrested to 'sanitize' the space for Olympics-goers until federal authorities issued a cease-and-desist order.[135] Some unhoused people were handed one-way bus tickets to faraway states.[136]

Like the Munich 1972 Olympics, the Atlanta Games were scarred by terrorism: a bomb cleaved through Centennial Olympic Park, killing one and wounding more than one hundred. At first, officials blamed security guard Richard Jewell, but in the end the bomber was proven to be Eric Robert Rudolph, an anti-abortion zealot who claimed the Olympics promoted the 'despicable ideals' of 'global socialism'.[137] At the closing ceremony, IOC President Samaranch insisted that '[n]o act of terrorism has ever destroyed the Olympic movement, and none ever will'.[138]

As noted in Chapter 1, in 1999 it emerged publicly that Salt Lake City's bid for the 2002 Winter Olympic was riddled with impropriety. Not only did the city's bid team hand over significant sums of cash to voting IOC members but, according to legal proceedings, it also laundered funds through 'a sham program … ostensibly to provide athletes in underprivileged countries with training and equipment'.[139] Needless to say, this was not the preamble to the 2000 Sydney Olympics that Games boosters envisioned.

Sydney Games organizers viewed environmental sustainability as 'one of the shining achievements' of the Olympics, 'a hallmark of Sydney's Games'.[140] They remediated a polluted industrial zone into a sparkling space, planted trees, and installed solar panels in the Olympic Village.[141] However, the Sydney Organizing Committee decided to stage the beach volleyball competition at Bondi Beach, an ecologically delicate location along the Pacific Ocean. Locals lost their beach access and wildlife was imperilled, but NBC, which had paid more than $600 million for broadcasting rights, desired Bondi Beach for its television-amenable scenery.[142] Activists from Bondi Olympic Watch fought back, burying themselves up to the neck in sand to thwart bulldozer operators, before they were dislodged by militarized security.[143]

The Sydney Olympics also touted its 'social sustainability', championing the success of Aboriginal track star Cathy Freeman. Not only did she light the Olympic cauldron at the opening ceremony, but she also went on to triumph in the 400-metre race. During her victory lap, she held aloft both the Aboriginal and Australian flags, a breach of Olympic protocol that the IOC opted to ignore.[144]

During the Sydney 2000 closing ceremony, Samaranch gushed, 'I am proud and happy to proclaim that you have presented to the world the best Olympic Games ever'.[145] And yet, Australian protesters exemplified a growing trend whereby activists used the Olympics as a stage for their political grievances, often attempting to piggyjack the Games – piggybacking off the Olympics' enormous audience while trying to hijack the platform for their own political messages. This continues today, as we shall see in Chapter 3, because of ongoing controversies around the Olympics in the 21st century.

3
PROBLEMS WITH
THE OLYMPICS

Partway through the 2022 Beijing Winter Olympics, 15-year-old Russian figure skater Kamila Valieva tested positive for a banned substance called trimetazidine, a heart medicine typically taken by older adults to treat coronary disease. The episode raised the spectre of the 2014 Sochi Winter Olympics where Russian athletes were involved in a state-sanctioned doping programme that was eventually revealed by Grigory Rodchenkov, a former director of Russia's anti-doping laboratory. The scandal read like a gripping spy novel. Rodchenkov described how the Russian Anti-Doping Agency teamed up with Russia's Federal Security Service – the successor to the KGB – to swap as many as one hundred clean urine samples through a small hole in the wall in order to cover up illegal doping. After Rodchenkov exposed the scheme, two members of the Russian anti-doping unit mysteriously dropped dead, even though both of them were healthy and in their fifties. The controversy rocked the Olympic world and threw into turmoil the World Anti-Doping Agency (WADA), which had failed to detect the comprehensive scheme.[1]

Journalists covering the 2022 Beijing Games not only connected the historical dots between Valieva's case and the previous state-sponsored plot, but also criticized the International Olympic Committee (IOC) for failing to protect athletes, especially teenagers like Valieva. *Washington Post* columnist Jerry Brewer slammed IOC President Thomas Bach for 'downplay[ing] the IOC's role in enabling the fiasco', writing that 'Olympic leadership failed Valieva, too, with its longtime cockamamie special treatment of a serial doping nation'.[2] After Russia's state-run doping programme was publicly exposed, the IOC allowed Russian athletes to continue to compete, although the country's anthem, flag, and name were barred. Instead, Russian Olympians participated as 'Olympic Athletes from Russia' at the 2018 Pyeongchang Winter Games and the 'Russian Olympic Committee' at the Tokyo 2020 Summer Olympics and the 2022 Beijing Games.

Russian doping is part of a longer history. In a high-performance sports world increasingly governed by the diktats of sport science, doping emerged as a vexing issue that continues to plague the Games. Performance-enhancing drugs have been studied since at least the 1870s, when Sir Robert Christison, the president of the British Medical Association, ran trials to gauge 'the restorative and preservative virtues of the

Peruvian cuca or coca-leaf against bodily fatigue from severe exercise'. After running tests on his students and himself, Christison concluded that chewing coca leaves 'removes extreme fatigue, and prevents it. Hunger and thirst are suspended. ... It has no effect on the mental faculties, so far as my own trials and other observations go, except liberating them from the dulness [sic] and drowsiness which follow great bodily fatigue'.[3] The early days of the Olympics featured athletes ingesting what they believed to be performance-enhancing substances, as when US marathoner Thomas Hicks gulped down brandy and microdoses of the highly toxic strychnine on his way to winning gold at the 1904 Games and when Dorando Pietri used strychnine in his unsuccessful bid to win the marathon at the 1908 Olympics.[4]

Since then, doping has not only become increasingly sophisticated, but also more politicized. After the Second World War, as the Cold War emerged and sport became a proxy battlefield for pre-eminence, anabolic steroids became a drug that weightlifters on either side of the Iron Curtain used to fast-track muscle growth. In East Germany, some 10,000 athletes were administered performance-enhancing drugs, with many – though not all – unaware of the drug experiments that sport scientists were running on them.[5] By 1956, even Pope Pius XII felt the need to comment – in the Bulletin du Comité International Olympique no less – condemning the use of 'gravely noxious substances' and 'highly stimulating drugs', which he viewed as 'a kind of fraud'.[6]

By the 1960s, athletes from numerous sports used steroids to bulk up, while others relied on amphetamines, especially in sports like cycling. At the 1960 Summer Games in Rome, Danish cyclist Knud Jensen fell from his bicycle and died; his autopsy revealed a cocktail of amphetamines that likely led to his death. This spurred IOC President Avery Brundage to initiate a doping commission, replete with a research team.[7] Drug testing was first introduced at the 1968 Winter Olympics in Grenoble, France and the Summer Games later that year in Mexico City. Since then, the Olympics have been in a high-tech cat-and-mouse game with athletes, trainers, and pharmacists, in part because of international prestige contests, but also due to the in-built incentive among Olympians to win glory. Four-time US Olympic hammer-thrower Harold 'Hal' Connolly made this crystal-clear in 1973 when he testified before the US Senate that 'the overwhelming majority of the international track and field athletes I have known would take anything and do anything short of killing themselves to improve their athletic performance'.[8]

The next decade, when Los Angeles hosted the 1984 Games, cross-cutting motivations were fully in play. According to doping scholar Thomas Hunt, some 'components of the Olympic governance system, including the IOC in the Los Angeles organizing committee, were motivated less by sincere concerns over doping than by economic issues'.[9] Such incentives exist today. WADA President Craig Reedie alleged that after his group chastised Russia for its widespread doping programme, IOC President Thomas Bach choreographed a 'pre-meditated campaign' comprised of 'personal attacks' that were meant to besmirch his reputation.[10]

When Canadian sprinter Ben Johnson was nabbed for steroids after he won gold in the 100-metre dash at the 1988 Seoul Olympics, it forced the IOC to ramp up its seriousness. But it wasn't until 1999 that it managed to help create WADA with a mandate to oversee a universal drug regulation strategy. WADA professionalized to an impressive degree, thanks in large part to the commitment and determination of IOC member Richard Pound. And yet, Hunt writes, 'a combination of organizational decentralization, venality, and individual indifference have seriously diminished the likelihood of an effective and sustained anti-doping policy'.[11]

While doping receives significant public attention, additional controversies have long swirled around the Olympics: astronomical spending, displacement of local people, the militarization of the public sphere, greenwashing, and corruption. These interlocked problems churn beneath the Olympics' shimmering surface in the 21st century, begetting a rising tide of public controversy. This chapter explores who benefits from the Olympics and who loses.

Olympic-sized spending

The Olympics have become notorious for costs that spiral ever upwards. I have previously called this dynamic Etch-A-Sketch economics, whereby during the Olympic bidding process Olympic supporters lowball costs only to have them escalate markedly by the time the Games are staged.[12] University of Oxford researchers analysed Olympics between 1960 and 2016 for which reliable data exist and found that every single Games ran over its initially stated budget, with an average cost overrun of 172 per cent in real terms, a notably higher mark-up rate than other mega-projects.[13] Olympic spending arrives with opportunity costs, too: money spent on the Games is not put towards socially productive activities like housing, education, and healthcare. In addition, the human power of politicians, their staff members, and urban planners are sunk into the Olympics rather than these socially beneficial areas. There can be a harrowing human toll to Olympic-style development, with sports funding propping up exploitative labour conditions as well as the army of volunteers upon whom the Games have become reliant.

Examples of Olympic overspending abound. The London 2012 Summer Games price tag started at $3.8 billion but ballooned to $18 billion. A Sky Sports investigation calculated the actual price tag, including necessary infrastructure projects, to be $38 billion. The 2014 Sochi Winter Olympics went from $12 billion to $51 billion, making the price of those Games higher than all previous Winter Olympics combined. The Rio 2016 Olympics went from $12 billion to $20 billion.[14] The cost of the 2018 Pyeongchang Games doubled from around $6 billion to $13 billion.[15] The Tokyo

Games were originally slated to cost $7.3 billion, but the price tag spiralled to around four times that, according to a government audit in Japan. COVID-19-induced postponement added billions more, bringing the total to around $30 billion.[16] Tokyo 2020's jaw-dropping cost overruns – well over 200 per cent – not only exceed the historical average for Olympic overspending, but make them the most expensive Summer Games to date.[17]

But overall costs only tell part of the story. Host cities are often left with white-elephant stadiums that are rarely used, but expensive to maintain. Olympic venues often slide into disrepair, forming grim monuments to misspending. For instance, the Pyeongchang downhill ski run sits rock-strewn and relatively unused. Meanwhile, Pyeongchang built a new stadium at a cost of $109 million that was originally slated for public use. However, it was used four times and then torn down in order to avoid creating a white elephant.[18] In Rio, numerous Olympic venues were abandoned after the Games as the country experienced an economic downturn. In Athens, the softball field and beach volleyball stadium from the 2004 Athens Summer Olympics were deserted, overgrown with weeds and strewn with trash, while the aquatic centre and canoe-slalom course are also derelict.[19] In Turin, host of the 2006 Winter Olympics, the Athletes Village was abandoned until refugees and migrants squatted in the facility and, working alongside enterprising advocates, eventually converted it into apartments, creating what was perhaps the most socially productive use of any Olympic venue.[20] Still, ghost venues haunt the Olympics.

The agreement that Olympic cities sign with the IOC typically place responsibility on the host for all cost overruns. In a scathing editorial, the Japanese newspaper *Asahi Shimbun* asserted that spiralling Tokyo 2020 Games costs were due in part to '[t]he unilateral nature of the host city contract signed with the International Olympic Committee' that placed too much power in the IOC's hands.[21] This chimes with an observation by Zev Yaroslavsky, the former LA city council member and Olympics supporter, who said in 2021:

> You don't sign a blank check to the International Olympic Committee if you are a steward of the taxpayers' money. You just can't do that. No private sector individual would ever have signed such a contract. And, in fact, when that contract was brought to the city, I took it ... to three of the most able and competent lawyers in Los Angeles in this field and I asked them 'what do you think?' and they said, 'I would never allow my client to sign such a contract'.[22]

The Los Angeles 2028 Olympics were originally supposed to cost $5.3 billion, but by April 2019, the price tag had already escalated to $6.9 billion.[23] Similarly, the Paris 2024 Games saw its costs leap from €6.8 billion in 2018 to €8.3 billion four years later, with some predicting they could leap to €10 billion by Games-time.[24]

Displacement: forced eviction and gentrification

The Olympics spur displacement. The general trend is that Olympic cities in the Global South experience displacement via the iron fist of forced eviction while hosts in the Global North face the velvet glove of gentrification. This issue especially affects working-class residents of Olympic cities. Public housing is often targeted for decimation to make way for Olympic venues, 'revitalized' neighbourhoods, and market-rate housing for upscale denizens.

The sheer number of people displaced by the Olympics can be jaw-dropping. Ahead of the 2008 Beijing Summer Olympics, more than a million people were dislodged from their homes to make way for the Games, according to the Geneva-based Centre on Housing Rights and Evictions (COHRE). This decimated the stockpile of affordable rental units, hurting local workers, many of whom were displaced without impartial consultation. COHRE found that 'many residents who left their homes "voluntarily" were, in fact, coerced into accepting compensation at rates that were not at the fair market value for homes in their neighbourhoods' even though this was required under Chinese law at the time.[25] Those who contested the unjust eviction process were dealt one-year 're-education through labour' sentences.[26] COHRE reported that Olympic organizers in coordination with municipal officials 'used tactics of harassment, repression, imprisonment, and even violence against residents and activists'.[27] One disgruntled Beijing resident who was forcibly evicted from his home told the *Washington Post*, '[t]he government always blames outsiders for politicizing the Olympics, but domestically they make the Olympics a political issue. We don't believe that our houses were torn down for the Olympics. The real purpose is moneymaking'.[28]

Ahead of the London 2012 Olympics, around 1,000 residents were displaced by the Games. Former British Olympian Sebastian Coe, who chaired the London Organizing Committee, promised in an essay titled 'It's Ludicrous to Claim the Olympics Will Lead to Evictions and Poverty' that the Games would rejuvenate East London and 'create between 30,000 and 40,000 new homes in the area'. Much of this housing stock, he promised, would be '"affordable housing" available to key workers such as nurses or teachers'.[29] Ten years later, only 13,000 homes had been built in the former Olympic zone, and only 11 per cent of those were affordable to working-class Londoners on average incomes.[30] 'Instead of being the diverse community that [was] promised, a model of social inclusion, we're getting the exact reverse', said one former member of the London Legacy Development Corporation.[31] Longtime residents in the five boroughs that hosted the Games saw their rents escalate, forcing them to move. In the years following the Olympics, Newham, one of the host boroughs, experienced the largest spike in home prices in all of London.[32] It also became the London borough with the highest rate of homelessness.[33]

Rio de Janeiro experienced intensive displacement ahead of the 2016 Summer Olympics, with 77,000 people evicted, many of them in favelas, the informal, high-density settlements with insecure property rights that span the city.[34] But amid the numbers one can lose sight of the fact that real people's lives are capsized. For example, there's Heloisa Helena Costa Berto, an Afro-Brazilian practitioner of the Candomblé religion who was evicted from Vila Autódromo, a working-class favela along the Jacarepaguá lagoon that was demolished to make space for a parking lot next to the Olympic media centre. Her whole life was overturned, including her religious practice, since the lagoon was home to her *orixá*, or deity.[35]

In Tokyo, developers used the state of exception brought by the 2020 Olympics to relax longtime height restrictions on construction in the neighbourhood around the National Stadium. In 1970 city officials in Tokyo instituted a 15-metre height limit, in part to prevent building higher than Meiji-era imperial structures. However, in 2013, to accommodate the new National Stadium design, the height restriction was erased and replaced with an 80-metre limit.[36] This regulation, made possible by the Olympics, pried open urban terrain for well-positioned real-estate firms to jump-start gentrification.

The change in zoning laws also cleared a political path for the elimination of public housing units. Residents from the Kasumigaoka apartment complex, which sat in the shadow of the new Olympic Stadium, were forced from public housing and relocated across the metropolis. Of the 370 residents who were evicted, 60 per cent were over 65 years old and many were widows in their eighties and nineties. Three people who lost their homes in Kasumigaoka were previously displaced by the 1964 Tokyo Olympics, too. One of those people, a woman in her sixties, said that '[t]he politicians don't listen. There is no political party willing to stand up to challenge Olympic priorities'. Meanwhile, benefiting from the new zoning codes, the Japanese Olympic Committee constructed a glassy tower near the stadium. High-end, high-rise apartment buildings were also built. In short, due to the Olympics, developers, landlords, and gentrifiers profited at the expense of the poor and elderly.[37] Such displacement, say critics, is low-intensity class warfare set to an upbeat, five-ring showtune.

Militarization of public space

National and local security and police forces use the Olympics like their own private cash machine, leveraging the Olympic state of exception to secure the funding, weapons, gear, and special laws that they would struggle to acquire during normal political times. Terrorism is real – just look at the Munich 1972 Olympics and the 1996 Atlanta Games – but when terrorists don't show up, activists do, and police have all sorts of tools at their disposal to squelch dissent and ensure that the sport spectacle proceeds. Also, everyday people in the Olympic city – especially communities of colour – are adversely affected by the militarized security build-up, with local police detaining, and sometimes arresting and jailing, locals in order to 'cleanse' the streets for the Olympic spectacle and the arrival of global Games-goers. The weapons secured for the Olympics are often used for racialized policing in the wake of the Games.

Organizers of the 2004 Athens Summer Games spent around $1.5 billion on security.[38] This amounted to $142,857 for each of the 10,500 athletes competing in Athens, or $283 for every ticket sold to an Olympic event. Even so, the IOC did not take any chances: for the first time ever, it purchased a pricey insurance policy for the Games' possible cancellation.[39] To be sure, this was the first Summer Olympics after the 9/11 terrorist attack, but local and national security officials exploited the Games as a once-in-a-generation opportunity to multiply and militarize their weapons stocks.

Athens security officials assembled what scholar Minas Samatas dubbed an 'Olympic superpanopticon' comprised of an array of sophisticated gear, including 'an electronic nexus of cameras, vehicle tracking devices, blimps, AWACS [Airborne Warning and Control System] airplanes, and satellites with continuous online linking by common databases and communications to provide real-time images and updates of available resources to a central command'. This was a 'military security umbrella' that required more than 70,000 military and security officials.[40] The militarized security system was not dismantled after the Games. A former minister of public order in Greece made this crystal-clear, writing that '[t]his great expenditure is not concerned only with the duration of the Olympics. It is an investment for the future'. He singled out '[t]he special training, technical know-how, and ultramodern equipment' that would transform 'the Hellenic Police into one of the best and most professional in the world'.[41]

Athens was no outlier. The Vancouver 2010 Winter Olympics security apparatus featured military-grade helicopters and CF-18 Hornet fighter jets. Police with semi-automatic weapons patrolled Olympic space, while more than 1,000 newly installed surveillance cameras blinked overhead across the city. Security officials even procured a Medium-Range Acoustic Device, battle-tested in war, although authorities were forced to disable its weapons function after pressure from civil libertarians.[42] None of this was cheap. Although the initial security budget was C$175 million, the price tag catapulted closer to C$1 billion.[43] Gord Hill, an Indigenous activist from the Kwakwaka'wakw Nation, described the process as 'police extortion from the ruling class'.[44]

To police the Olympics, the government formed a new body: the Vancouver Integrated Security Unit (VISU), which was led by the Royal Canadian Mounted Police and comprised more than 20 police agencies – including the Canadian Security Intelligence Service and the Department of National Defence – totalling more than 17,000 security officials in all. One-fifth of the entire country's policing power saturated Vancouver for the Olympic moment, including 6,000 officers from more than 100 police departments. VISU also included around 5,000 military personnel, more than the 2,900 Canadian troops stationed in Afghanistan at the time. It collaborated with the FBI and the Department of Homeland Security in the US to create an 'Olympics Coordination Center' in Bellingham, Washington.[45]

Ahead of the Games, the City of Vancouver passed a '2010 Winter Games By-law' prohibiting posters, placards, and banners that were not 'celebratory' (although it was legal to raise 'a sign that celebrates the 2010 Winter Games, and creates or enhances a festive environment and atmosphere'). The ordinance criminalized anti-Olympics signs and provided Canadian security officials with the right to remove them, even if that meant confiscating them on private property. To raise awareness, local artist Jesse Corcoran painted a mural featuring the five Olympic rings encircling four frowny faces and one smiley face, installing outside the Crying Room Gallery in Vancouver (see Figure 3.1). Corcoran said at the time: 'The oppressive nature of the Games is what I wanted to capture and how the majority is suffering for the minority.'[46] The mural attracted the attention of local police, who insisted it violated the 'Sign By-Law' and needed to be taken down. After a legal battle, city officials backpedalled.[47]

At the London 2012 Olympics, security officials fastened surface-to-air missiles onto the rooftop of a housing complex where everyday Londoners lived. The military was ubiquitous on the streets after it was forced to supply security when the private firm G4S failed to provide the trained staff they promised. In Russia, whip-wielding Cossack militia members took to the streets to preserve order, attacking the

Figure 3.1: Anti-Olympics mural in Vancouver, Canada

This mural was painted by local artist Jesse Corcoran and installed outside the Crying Room Gallery ahead of the 2010 Winter Games.

art-activist collective Pussy Riot when they performed in public space. In Rio, 85,000 security personnel were put to work, double the number in London (see Figure 3.2).[48] Moreover, Rio Olympic bidders conflated terrorism and activism; their bid book contained a section titled 'Activist/Terrorist Risks' even though they conceded that '[t]he risk to the Games from protest action and domestic terrorism is low'. The bid specifically identified 'issue motivated groups' that are 'concerned with indigenous rights, environmental or anti-globalization issues'.[49]

In 2017, Japanese legislators rammed anti-terrorism legislation through the parliament, justifying its hasty passage by claiming the need to securitize the Tokyo 2020 Olympics. The legislation added hundreds of new crimes to Japanese law, including offences such as sit-ins to oppose the construction of new apartment buildings.[50] Similarly, the French National

Figure 3.2: Police presence at the Rio Games

Police were ubiquitous at the 2016 Rio Olympics, with more than 85,000 security personnel in action, double the number at the London 2012 Olympics.

Assembly used the Olympic state of exception to approve the experimental use of AI-driven video surveillance at the Paris 2024 Olympics. The law permits video surveillance guided by AI algorithms to detect 'suspicious' or 'abnormal' activity in Olympic crowds, analysing video data from drones and fixed CCTV cameras and notifying police. The law will stay in place through March 2025, long after the Olympics have concluded, a reminder that new laws and weapons secured for the Games are often used in everyday policing after the event, sometimes becoming the new normal.[51]

Greenwashing

Beginning in the 1990s, the IOC made sustainability a new arrow in its rhetorical quiver. Environmental concerns – such as the perils of climate change – were seeping their way into mainstream discourse, aided by both a burgeoning global environmental movement and the United Nations' publicly stated commitment to preserving the Earth. In 1992, after the UN's high-profile 'Earth Summit', the IOC followed suit with a symbolic 'Earth Pledge' with the stated aim of 'making the Earth a safe place'.[52] However, as Christine O'Bonsawin, an Indigenous sport scholar and a member of the Abenaki Nation at Odanak, notes, Olympic power brokers often craft a 'sustainability smokescreen' instead of creating meaningful environmental and social sustainability programmes.[53] In other words, IOC luminaries have veered towards greenwashing, the duplicitous practice of voicing concern for the environment and claiming credit for providing solutions while doing the bare minimum, if anything, to make material ecological improvements. With greenwashing, symbolism trumps substance.

One systematic, longitudinal assessment of Olympic sustainability at 16 installations of the Summer and Winter Games between 1992 through 2020 found a sizable gap between IOC rhetoric and reality. The authors broadened the discussion of sustainability, parcelling it into three types: ecological, social, and economic. In terms of environmental sustainability, they factored in the amount of fresh construction, the ecological footprint of Olympic visitors, and the size of the Games. Overall, the researchers found that the Olympic Games achieved 'medium' sustainability marks, earning 48 out of 100 points on their nine-indicator scale. With the ecological dimension, host cities averaged 44 points, while the mean for social and economic sustainability were 51 and 47 respectively. Notably, the scholars concluded that Olympic-style sustainability diminished over time, with the environmental dimension decreasing the most. As the IOC ramped up its environmental sustainability rhetoric, its follow-through weakened. 'The promotion of the environment and sustainability to a pillar of the Olympic policy agenda', the authors concluded, 'has not been able to stop or reverse the decline of sustainability over time'.[54]

The researchers found that the 2002 Salt Lake City Winter Games were the most sustainable during the time period under study. Meanwhile, the four least sustainable Olympics – the 2014 Sochi Winter Olympics, the 2016 Summer Games in Rio de Janeiro, the 2020 Tokyo Olympics, and the London 2012 Games – were quite recent, pointing up the inconvenient fact that the Olympics have not consistently improved their sustainability follow-through over time.[55] Nevertheless, IOC officials continue to tout their sustainability promises, sometimes in concert with partners like the United Nations, as when, in December 2022, they trumpeted a UN General Assembly resolution declaring 'sport as an enabler of sustainable development'.[56]

Mega-events scholar Martin Müller writes that '[t]he grand claim to organise "the greenest Games ever"' has become 'almost de rigueur for mega-event hosts', even though it so often 'rings hollow'.[57] Zooming in on sustainability practices at recent installations of the Olympics supports Müller's observation that a chasm exists between green word and deed. For the 2010 Winter Olympics, Vancouver built a Sea-to-Sky highway link to venues in Whistler, even though it jeopardized animal life, including endangered species like the red-legged frog.[58] At the London 2012 Olympics, organizers created a new category of corporate sponsor: 'sustainability partners'. They included BP as well as BMW, BT, Cisco, EDF Energy and GE. An independent watchdog group – the Commission for a Sustainable London 2012 – revealed that the sponsorship programme was simply a pay-to-play charade. In truth, no environmental standards needed to be met in order to become a 'sustainability partner'.[59]

The 2014 Sochi Games led to irreversible environmental destruction and, due to sub-standard governance, failed to meet the sustainability goals delineated in the original bid.[60] Although the bid books for the Rio 2016 Olympics vowed to clean up the notoriously polluted Guanabara Bay – which hosted the Olympic sailing and windsurfing competitions – by treating more than 80 per cent of the sewage that flowed into the Bay, this never transpired. Ahead of the Games, an Associated Press investigation revealed that every single water venue was unsafe; waterways were riddled with human waste that delivered perilously high levels of viruses and bacteria. Ingesting merely three teaspoons of the polluted water afforded a 99 per cent chance of a viral infection (although that did not mean someone would automatically fall ill). Even contracting hepatitis A was a possibility. By the time the Games began, around 169 million gallons of untreated sewage continued to gurgle into Guanabara Bay each day.[61]

For the Pyeongchang 2018 Winter Games, South Korean bidders promised that they would deliver a 'Green Dreams' Olympics featuring 'the most advanced, environmentally friendly strategies'. Then they chopped down 58,000 trees in a sacred 500-year-old forest on Mount Gariwang to make way for an Olympic ski run.[62] The IOC's 'Sustainability and Legacy Commission' remained silent in the face of this forest destruction. Researcher Jung Woo Lee found that the Pyeongchang Games actually achieved 'economic and ecological *unsustainability*' and that 'the economic and ecological problems caused by the Olympic development are still on-going'.[63] Four years later, for the Beijing 2022 Winter Games, organizers sliced an alpine ski run through the pristine Yanqing Songshan National Forest Park, home to numerous rare species, including Beijing's only Shanxi orchids.[64] Then, Games planners used artificial snow, gobbling up previous water supplies in a parched part of the country, exacerbating the greenwash.[65]

The Tokyo 2020 Summer Olympics merit special attention for the Games' extraordinary greenwashing. During the bid phase, Prime Minister Shinzo Abe assured jittery IOC voters that everything was 'under control' after Fukushima Prefecture was slammed by a tsunami, earthquake and nuclear meltdown in

2011. Then, Games organizers rhetorically prioritized ecological renewal by adopting a 'Recovery Olympics' slogan that pledged the Olympics would aid the clean-up. However, Japan-based scholar Satoko Itani disputed this, stating ahead of the Games: 'This Olympics is literally taking the money, workers, and cranes away from the areas where they are needed most.'[66] Japanese social critic Koide Hiroaki framed the situation in clear moral terms: 'The Tokyo Olympics [would] take place in a state of nuclear emergency. Those countries and people who participate will, on the one hand, themselves risk exposure, and, on the other, become accomplices to the crimes of this nation.'[67]

When I visited Fukushima in July 2019, my group was accompanied by scientist and professor Fujita Yasumoto, who carried a hand-held dosimeter, a device that measures external ionizing radiation levels. As we travelled through Fukushima Prefecture, the dosimeter readings elevated, eventually reaching a zenith at the TEPCO decommissioning archive centre and museum where radiation levels were 18 times higher than the recommended standard. While there, I spoke with Masumi Kowata, an elected official on the Okuma Town city council. She eviscerated Abe's 'under control' comment, rebuking the Olympics' recovery narrative: 'Things are absolutely not "under control" and nothing is over yet. The nuclear radiation is still very high. Only one small section is being cleaned. The wider region is still an evacuation zone. There is still radiation in the area.' She explained how in Fukushima, residents were encouraged to return to their homes even though the federal government had plans to eliminate property-tax exemptions for residents in Kowata's district after the Olympics, meaning homeowners would have to resume paying taxes on uninhabitable homes in towns to which they could not safely return.[68] *Scientific American* concluded that 'Abe's determination to put the Daiichi accident behind the nation is jeopardizing public health, especially among children, who are more susceptible'.[69]

As we manoeuvred through the towns of Fukushima Prefecture, we passed thousands of sizable plastic bags that were piled into what locals called 'black pyramids' – enormous stacks of plastic bags containing radioactive topsoil (see Figure 3.3). Men donning jumpsuits and paper masks were filling, hauling, and stacking the contaminated soil. Trucks transported some bags away to distant areas; we saw dozens of these pyramids along the side of the highway. Many of the bags were bursting as seedlings sprouted through the plastic. When it was windy, the contaminated soil blew into the air. When a typhoon struck Japan in October 2019, some of the bags from the black pyramids washed into nearby rivers.[70] In this context, Fukushima can be viewed as a 'sacrifice zone', a term that emerged during the Cold War to denote a space made unliveable by nuclear fallout.[71] In some ways, the Tokyo Olympics contributed to making Fukushima a capitalist sacrifice zone for the climate-change era.[72]

Meanwhile, the US-based non-governmental organization Rainforest Action Network detailed how Korindo, a Tokyo 2020 wood supplier, engaged

Figure 3.3: 'Black pyramids' in Fukushima, Japan, July 2019

The black pyramids consisted of black plastic bags containing topsoil at various stages of radioactivity.

in unsustainable practices and illegal behaviour that fuelled forest destruction in Indonesia. Wood used to build numerous Olympic venues was unethically sourced.[73] In March 2020, eight environmental non-governmental organizations issued a joint statement slamming Tokyo 2020 organizers for 'fake sustainability'. They asserted that 'Tokyo 2020's use of large quantities of tropical plywood linked to rainforest destruction for construction of the Olympic venues was a clear violation of its commitment to sustainability'.[74] In sum, Tokyo 2020 shows how the IOC's rhetorical attention to ecological concerns has become a go-to method for embracing the global zeitgeist of environmentalism while anaesthetizing the public to the deleterious impacts of the Olympics.[75]

Democracy deficit and corruption

The Olympics can short-circuit democratic practice. The Olympic state of exception creates space for Games organizers and local politicians to undercut typical democratic procedures during both the bid process and the delivery phase of the Games. Once the mega-event is allocated to a city, countless staff hours are gobbled up by Olympic matters, often deflecting attention from pressing social problems. Moreover, the elected officials who sign the host-city contract are typically long gone by the time the Olympics arrive, thereby undercutting democratic accountability.

All these dynamics were in play when Los Angeles was bidding on the 2024 – and then eventually, the 2028 – Olympics. As described in the Introduction, the Los Angeles City Council vote to authorize mayor Eric Garcetti to sign a host-city contract with the IOC was preordained, with only pro-Games voices allowed to testify while critics were sidelined. During a subcommittee meeting ahead of the vote, City Council member Joe Buscaino thundered, 'I'm getting tired of people standing up and questioning our decision-making'. An activist from the anti-Games group NOlympics LA retorted, 'It's called democracy!' Buscaino then angrily stammered, 'What these Games will do is create jobs and weed out poverty and put Los Angeles on the map'.[76] To activists, 'weeding out poverty' was a cipher for stoking gentrification and displacement. And wasn't Los Angeles already 'on the map'?

Neither the word 'democracy' nor 'democratic' appear in the host-city contract between the IOC and LA. And US courts do not have jurisdiction over disagreements between LA organizers and the IOC. Instead, the pact states that '[t]he obligations of the Parties under the HCC [host-city contract] shall be defined, first, by the terms of the HCC, second, by the terms of the Olympic Charter and, third, by application of the principles of interpretation of Swiss law'.[77] Mayor Garcetti will not have to deal with any such disagreements: he departed office in December 2022.

The IOC itself has in recent years become less democratic and less transparent. The group makes more decisions behind closed doors and hunkers around an increasingly iron-fisted president in Thomas Bach. Under Bach's leadership, the IOC has turned a blind eye to political repression in Olympic host cities and countries, thereby enabling sportswashing: when political leaders use sports to appear important or legitimate on the world stage while stirring nationalism and deflecting attention from chronic problems and human-rights issues at home.[78] In reality, the IOC has started to resemble the very authoritarian governments that it is not only unwilling to criticize, but with whom it openly collaborates. German investigative journalist Jens Weinreich, an Olympic watchdog for more than three decades, stated that '[t]he IOC itself is a totalitarian system. More than ever'.[79] In 2021, after

Bach announced that he would run for re-election, IOC members, one after the other, heaped histrionic praise on him, with one saying, 'We have one captain, and that captain is you'. In such a 'culture of deference', as the *New York Times* put it, Bach was re-elected with dictator numbers: 93–1 with four abstentions.[80]

Unchecked autocracy is a recipe for corruption. With all the money sloshing through the Olympic system, the Games have long been plagued by corruption, both during the bid process and Games delivery. The Tokyo 2020 Olympics and their aftermath crystallize these dynamics. According to a Reuters investigation, Haruyuki Takahashi took $8.2 million from the Tokyo bid committee to procure IOC votes. Although the former executive at the formidable Japanese advertising agency Dentsu denied wrongdoing, he admitted that he lobbied influential IOC members like Lamine Diack. (Beginning in 2015, Diack, the former head of the international governing body for track and field, lived under house arrest in France on corruption charges and accusations that he concealed failed drug tests and blackmailed athletes. He died in December 2021.) Takahashi conceded that he provided gifts to Diack – like cameras and a Seiko watch – but that when it came to persuading IOC members, this was simply business as usual: 'You don't go empty-handed. That's common sense', he said.[81]

Takahashi was integrated into the Tokyo bid unit by Tsunekazu Takeda, then head of the enterprise. Takeda is the son of former IOC member Prince Tsuneyoshi Takeda and the great-grandson of the Emperor Meiji, ruler of Japan from 1867 to 1912. Takeda was indicted in January 2019 on corruption charges related to $2 million in payments he allegedly okayed for Black Tidings, a Singapore-based company overseen by Papa Massata Diack, the son of Lamine Diack. While Takeda insists these payments were for consulting work, French authorities consider them bribes meant for the elder Diack. In mid-2019, Takeda resigned from the Japanese Olympic Committee, claiming innocence.[82]

The delivery of the Tokyo Games was also mired in serious corruption allegations. Japanese prosecutors even arrested Takahashi, the former Dentsu executive, accusing him of accepting bribes for Olympic contracts from numerous firms: a publishing company that printed Olympic programmes, a doll-maker that produced stuffed-animal mascots, and a clothing firm that made Games uniforms. Even Seiko Hashimoto, the head of the Tokyo 2020 Organizing Committee, admitted that '[t]he significance and value of the Tokyo Games have come into question'.[83]

'We want the [Olympic] legacy to be different', stated the president of the Paris 2024 Olympics, three-time Olympic gold-medal-winner in canoe slalom Tony Estanguet. However, when it comes to corruption, the Paris Games actually might not be so different. In June 2023, French financial police raided and searched the headquarters of the Paris 2024 Olympics, reportedly related to two separate investigations into the awarding of public contracts.[84]

Inveterate IOC critic Andrew Jennings likened the IOC to organized crime, with both guided by 'the *omertà* culture'. The IOC and the mafia, he argued, both operate under a code of silence and are typified by 'a strong and ruthless leader, a hierarchy, a strong code of conduct for its members and, above all, the goal of power and profit'.[85] Not all IOC members skate away free. In 2021, self-suspended IOC member Carlos Nuzman, who headed the Rio 2016 Olympics and the Brazilian Olympic Committee, was convicted on charges of money laundering, corruption, and additional crimes and sentenced to more than 30 years in prison.[86]

Anti-Olympics activism

These consistent Olympic downsides create what Rob Nixon calls 'slow violence', or 'a violence that occurs gradually and out of sight, a violence of delayed destruction that is dispersed across time and space, an attritional violence that is typically not viewed as violence at all'.[87] This 'slow violence' has earned intensified scrutiny in the media and among academics and human-rights workers. It has also galvanized anti-Olympics activism in cities around the world.[88] For instance, after Julian Cheyne was displaced from Clays Lane housing estate in East London to make way for the 2012 Games, he responded by becoming a prolific anti-Olympics activist, founding the Counter-Olympics Network and Games Monitor, two watchdog websites.[89]

Recent years have brought an uptick in anti-Olympics activism across the globe. Anti-Games activism in Tokyo involved two central groups: Hangorin no Kai and OkotowaLink. Hangorin no Kai, which translates to 'Anti-Olympics Group', engaged in numerous protests in the years leading up to the Tokyo Games. The group was born in 2013 and has a firm core of around a dozen active members, with numbers climbing towards 100 for creative, playful protests and street actions.[90] OkotowaLink, which roughly translates to 'No Thanks Olympics 2020', is packed with academics and researchers who double as political organizers. In July 2019 these groups teamed up with anti-Olympics activists from around the world for the first-ever anti-Olympics summit. The week-long series of events included strategy-sharing sessions, public

Figure 3.4: Activists in Tokyo attend a rally before marching through the Shinjuku District, July 2019

talks, and tours of Olympic areas. There was also a large mobilization in the Shinjuku district of Tokyo that garnered around 1,000 participants (see Figure 3.4). Hangorin no Kai and OkotowaLink were joined by dissidents from recent host cities like Pyeongchang, Rio de Janeiro, and London as well as future hosts like Paris and Los Angeles. The summit overlapped the one-year mark before the original start date for the Tokyo Summer Olympics: 24 July 2020.[91]

Then, in May 2022, anti-Olympics activists in Paris organized a second transnational anti-Games summit, convening dissidents from cities bidding on

Figure 3.5: Anti-Games activists

Activists from around the world convene in Paris for the second-ever transnational anti-Olympics summit in May 2022. From left to right: Frédéric Viale, Maria Escobet, and Natsuko Sasaki.

the Games as well as past and future host cities (see Figure 3.5). Instead of temporarily assembling extant groups in the Olympic city that are already fighting police militarization, gentrification, and greenwashing only to have them melt back into their original activist tracks after the Games take place, organizers are trying to create an anti-Olympics movement that can hop from site to site. They are trying to build an enduring *movement* of movements rather than a *moment* of movements that work together in the short term.[92]

Anne Orchier, an organizer with NOlympics LA who was part of the contingent of activists who travelled to Tokyo in July for the inaugural transnational summit, said: 'We have always known that Olympic organizers prioritize their profit margins over human life, putting both athletes and residents of host cities at considerable risk in order to squeeze out an extra million here and there.'[93] These sentiments have gained traction in numerous cities bidding on the Olympics, forcing the IOC to adjust its approach. Chapter 4 analyses recent Olympic reforms and what needs to be done to transform the Games into a force for social good.

4

CAN THE OLYMPICS BE FIXED?

S tanding in front of more than 100 International Olympic Committee (IOC) members who had gathered in Monaco for official meetings, IOC President Thomas Bach recognized that in order for the Olympics to remain relevant and to fend off mounting criticism, the Games needed to reform. 'If we do not address these challenges here and now we will be hit by them very soon', he said. 'If we do not drive these changes ourselves, others will drive us to them. We want to be the leaders of change in sport, not the object.' Bach implored, 'The time for change is now.'[1]

It was 2014 and the IOC president was facing the reality that numerous potential host cities were jilting the Olympics at the bidding altar. Bach uttered his admonition after several prospective hosts for the 2022 Winter Olympics dropped out – including Oslo, Stockholm, Kraków, and Lviv, Ukraine – leaving only Beijing and Almaty, Kazakhstan in the running. Around the world, more and more people were arriving at the conclusion that although the Olympics *appear* to be for athletes and public enjoyment, behind the thin scrim of Olympism lurks brass-knuckle money-machinations, endemic downsides for the Olympic host city, and the ever-voracious IOC, a group increasingly perceived as prioritizing its own interests and survival over the wellbeing of athletes and the host city. Between 2013 and 2018 alone, more than a dozen cities terminated their Olympic bids, after losing a public referendum, merely facing the prospect of a public vote, or succumbing to political pressure against the Games.[2]

Upon being elected president in 2013, Bach initially sliced against Olympic tradition, stating: 'The IOC cannot be apolitical.' He added: 'We have to realize that our decisions at events like [the] Olympic Games, they have political implications. And when taking these decisions we have to, of course, consider political implications.'[3] However, by 2020, Bach had U-turned, reverting to the time-worn IOC stance that politics and the Olympics shouldn't mix. He railed against 'the growing politicisation of sport', asserting: 'As history has shown, such politicisation of sport leads to no result and in the end just deepens existing divisions.'[4]

Ahead of the Beijing 2022 Winter Olympics, Bach clung to this brand of apoliticism, refusing to comment on the treatment of Uyghurs in Xinjiang Province, stating: 'There the position of the IOC must be, given the political neutrality, that we're not commenting on political issues.' Journalist Christine Brennan skewered

Bach for his stance: 'The IOC has played this game for years, saying it's neutral when it's wheeling and dealing behind the scenes with some of the world's greatest scoundrels to force them to pay up to host the Olympics.' Brennan added, 'But this moment of IOC pomposity was the most breathtaking yet: The president of the IOC passed on genocide as just another issue on which to sit on the fence.'[5]

Months later, though, Bach rebuked Russian athletes who openly showed support for the invasion of Ukraine by donning the 'Z' symbol during international competition. This followed the IOC's demand – driven by political considerations – that all international sports federations ban athletes from Russia and Belarus after

Figure 4.1: Across the world, the Uyghur community protested against the Beijing 2022 Winter Olympics

This photo is from a demonstration in Amsterdam on 5 February 2022.

Russia, with the support of Belarus, invaded Ukraine in February 2022. When asked why the IOC weighed in while remaining silent about other military skirmishes that raged around the world, Bach stated that '[t]he war in Ukraine is different because it is a blatant violation of the Olympic Truce', asserting that 'the far-reaching political, social and economic consequences of the war make it a turning point in world history'.[6] This quirky political determination was not only inconsistent – Bach did not penalize Russia when it invaded Crimea between the 2014 Sochi Olympics and Paralympics – but it also undercut the IOC's claims of apoliticism.

As the Paris 2024 Summer Olympics approached, the IOC carved a path for the participation of athletes from Russia and Belarus, arguing that '[n]o athlete should be prevented from competing just because of their passport'.[7] And yet, Russian President Vladimir Putin has long put the Olympics towards political propaganda purposes. The Russian military's decimation of several Ukrainian sports facilities and its killing of numerous Ukrainian athletes amid the invasion does not sync up with Principle 4 of the Olympic Charter: 'Every individual must have the possibility of practising sport, without discrimination of any kind and in the Olympic spirit, which requires mutual understanding with a spirit of friendship, solidarity and fair play.'[8] The IOC's slippery stance sparked sharp reactions. A Ukrainian presidential aide thundered that the 'IOC is a promoter of war, murder and destruction. The IOC watches with pleasure Russia destroying Ukraine and then offers Russia a platform to promote genocide and encourages their further killings'.[9] The threat of a boycott loomed.

This book has examined how the IOC's self-proclaimed aversion to politics has long not stood up to scrutiny. In reality, the IOC could use a walk-in closet for all its political skeletons. Theirs is 'an apoliticism that is in fact deeply political', as Theodor Adorno would have it.[10] A first step towards meaningfully reforming the Olympics would be for the IOC to ditch the durable myth that the Olympics are not political. Admitting that they are indeed political would allow the IOC to take resolute, principled action when the Games are used to advance politics that are drenched in hate or that clash with stated Olympic ideals. Claiming to transcend politics means forfeiting the chance to stand up for justice in ways that chime with the Olympic Charter. The IOC's brand of apoliticism does not indicate neutrality. It points up an abdication of responsibility. And it severely limits the IOC's ability to fix the Olympics.

Olympic reform

When Thomas Bach initially called for reform in 2014, many Olympics watchers were optimistic that a significant change in course was imminent. Bach arrived in Monaco with a slate of recommendations – called 'Olympic Agenda 2020' – that the IOC adopted unanimously and that boosters promoted as a game-changer. The main aims included reshaping the Olympic bidding process to reduce costs, bolstering the IOC's commitment to sustainability, reconsidering the sports programme while pressing towards gender equity, integrating corporate sponsors more fully into Olympic programming, and initiating an Olympic television channel to maximize fan engagement between Games.[11] As a set of recommendations, 'Olympic Agenda 2020' required conversion into IOC policy.

Then in 2018, the IOC issued its 'New Norm' programme that – drawing from principles nestled in Olympic Agenda 2020 – pinpointed potential adjustments to the bidding process for and organization of the Games, with an eye on reducing overall costs.[12] Taken together, these programmes sought to streamline the complex process of Games delivery while initiating greater flexibility that shifted power towards the host city. Scholar Sven Daniel Wolfe distils the reforms into three key areas: governance, infrastructures, and transparency. 'Governance refers to widening the circle of those who participate in decision-making, including a greater diversity of local stakeholders and experts', he writes. 'Infrastructures refer to the ways in which the event should take advantage of existing facilities, aligning with the city's long-term development agenda. And transparency means that development plans should be conducted and executed ethically and openly.'[13]

Through the reform process, the IOC encouraged prospective host cities to engage in low-key, non-committal discussions before plunging full-bore into an official bid. The IOC also promoted the use of existing sports facilities while showing openness to modular or temporary venues as well as Olympic facilities outside the geographical boundaries of the host city.[14] Reforms were meant to address the criticism, voiced by an IOC manager, that '[i]n the past, we used to come in and somehow impose our will onto the city. ... Today it is very much the Games that adapt to the city. That's very different in how we work, and that's probably the single biggest challenge we have'.[15]

In 2019, the IOC approved the creation of two permanent Future Host Commissions, one each for the Summer and Winter Olympics. These commissions are designed to 'permanently explore, monitor and encourage interest in future Olympics Games' while engaging with the IOC's Executive Board.[16] The Summer Olympics Commission consists of up to ten IOC members and the Winter Commission is limited to eight or fewer individuals. Commissions are comprised of a range of Olympic actors, from representatives of International Federations (IFs) and National Olympic Committees (NOCs) to members of the International Paralympic Committee and the IOC Athletes' Commission. The Commissions are permitted to visit prospective hosts, 'if required', even though reforms instituted after the Salt Lake City bribery scandal forbade site visits in order to prevent corruption.[17] While the creation of Future Host Commissions decreases pressure on potential hosts and infuses the process with reciprocal cooperation, these less-formal dynamics, according to organizational theory scholars, can potentially lead to 'social bribes' whereby 'socially bounded' agents and clients 'informally exchange resources, but the gift or countergift does not come from the agent's own pocket but from the public organization' they represent. One public-administration scholar proposed that with social bribes 'between closely connected partners, strong informal norms extinguish internal and external top-down rule-based policies', thereby widening the path towards corruption.[18]

In February 2021, the IOC issued a 37-page report – 'Olympic Agenda 2020+5: 15 Recommendations' – that celebrated how the Olympic Movement was 'turning challenges into opportunities' and offered recommendations (such as deepening engagement with the burgeoning video-gaming community), many of which mirrored previously articulated aspirations. Veteran Olympics-watcher David Owen wondered aloud whether 'the resuscitated roadmap isn't more of a security blanket, a way of trying to kid yourself and others that you are more in control than you actually are'.[19] Then, in March, the IOC issued its closing report on Agenda 2020, breaking down what the IOC had achieved since the ideas were first proposed. Bach heralded 'Agenda 2020' as an unequivocal success, concluding: 'Our reforms have of course not only impacted the international community at large, but first and foremost, they have changed our Olympic community.'[20]

Yet Wolfe argues that '[d]espite making significant improvements in regards to power sharing with local authorities, the series of Olympic reforms so far fails to give adequate voice to residents. There is a disjuncture between the goals of the reforms and the outcomes on the ground'. He adds, '[u]ltimately, without a broader assemblage of stakeholders that better includes affected residents, Olympic reforms risk repeating the crises of social and spatial exclusion that they were ostensibly designed to solve'.[21] In other words, Olympic reforms left unaddressed many of the ingrained controversies that dog the Games, as discussed in Chapter 3: overspending, displacement, police militarization, greenwashing, and corruption. Thus, many reform-minded critics argue that the IOC had not gone far enough.

Charting change

The IOC is an insulated enclave of power conspicuously committed to policing its own behaviour. Although the IOC has cultivated strong relationships with outside groups like the United Nations and the World Health Organization, these groups do not exert the necessary leverage to truly reform the Olympic Games. Neither does the IOC's Ethics Commission: it reports to the IOC's Executive Board and does not have independent sanction power.[22] Oversight carried out by independent bodies *outside* the Olympic Movement – such as an autonomous inspector general with investigative powers to probe misconduct in the Olympics sphere, or a toothy 'climate regulator' to assess green claims[23] – is the firmest path towards accountability. This must be a bedrock principle for any serious set of Olympic reforms. Until this happens, the IOC will remain open to the charge that it is the most expansive yet least accountable sport infrastructure in the world.

Some cling to the notion that meaningful, structural change can originate from inside the 'Olympic family'. And yet, Richard Pound, the most senior member of the IOC, said before his retirement in 2022, 'I paid the price for publicly expressed opposition to the IOC's decisions, through my removal as chairman of OBS [Olympic Broadcasting Services], as director of OCS [Olympic Channel Services] and from the Legal Affairs Commission'.[24] If Pound – who one Olympic insider views as 'the most important member in the ... history of sport's most exclusive club not to have been installed as President' – faced retribution from the IOC, an organization to which he had dedicated most of his adult life, then how can we expect lesser-experienced IOC members – let alone an athlete or group of athletes – to work from the inside to change this formidable behemoth?[25]

Every two years, as the Olympics approach and chronic problems linked to the Games emerge in the public sphere, two common solutions are offered:

1. permanently site the Olympics in a single location;
2. rotate hosting duties for both the summer and winter Olympics among a small number of cities that have previously staged the Games.

Setting aside the fact that the IOC has shown zero interest in either proposal, as neither would quench its thirst for new markets, it's not clear that there would be a lot of takers on the host side. Everyday people in Athens – which is often mentioned as a permanent site for the Summer Olympics, given its historical importance – may not be overly keen; after all, the Athens 2004 Games were a budget-buster that created a herd of white-elephant stadiums and opened the door to intensified surveillance.[26] On the surface, rotating Olympic cities might reduce fresh construction, but given the ever-evolving standards for stadiums, this might not actually be the case. After all, the Georgia Dome, built in 1992 and used at the 1996 Atlanta Games, became an architectural fossil and was rubbled only 25 years later.[27] Complicating matters, the Winter Olympics can feasibly be staged in fewer and fewer locations because of climate change, a fate that may well affect Summer Games soon, too.[28]

With this in mind, there are three key reforms that could stimulate meaningful change in the Olympics:

1. installing and enforcing rigorous human-rights standards;
2. fostering real-deal athlete power; and
3. infusing democracy into Olympic policies and processes.

Human rights

Were the IOC to abide and enforce human-rights standards – in regards to both host cities and countries as well as athletes – they could make important strides towards justice. The IOC appears to realize that human rights are important. The Olympic Charter heralds sport's role in promoting human rights and ethics. One 'fundamental principle of Olympism' states that '[t]he practice of sport is a human right'. Another trumpets 'the harmonious development of humankind, with a view to promoting a peaceful society concerned with the preservation of human dignity'.[29]

And yet, the Beijing 2022 Olympics highlighted the IOC's willingness to overlook serious human-rights abuses in the host country. IOC Vice President Juan Antonio Samaranch made it crystal-clear that the IOC would not press China on human-rights issues, and only address rights 'in the context of the Olympic Games'. He contended: 'We cannot go further than that. ... Not here, not anywhere else. If we would start doing that we would be in serious trouble because there is always someone that doesn't like something that the other did. It's a very fine line and a very complex issue.'[30] Unfortunately, the IOC has responded to the human-rights quandary not as an impetus for deep reflection and meaningful action but instead as a public-relations puzzle requiring freshened messaging and retrenched pseudo-apoliticism. This must change.

The stakes are high. 'Whatever the human rights problems are before a major sporting event like the Olympics are awarded, they will be seriously exacerbated by a multi-billion-dollar sporting event', said Minky Worden, the Director of Global Initiatives at Human Rights Watch. The Games have 'a metastasizing effect' on rights abuses: 'The overarching trend is that if the human-rights conditions are poor in a country, not only will the Olympics not change them, it will make them much worse.'[31] Andrea Florence, the Brazilian lawyer who directs the Sport and Rights Alliance, pointed to the 'IOC's historical reluctance to recognize its responsibility to respect human rights'. When sports governing bodies do adopt human-rights policies, she said that all too often they 'don't acknowledge violations, provide any guarantees of non-repetition, or compensate people, workers, women, or children who are negatively affected by their events'.[32]

In September 2022 – *after* the 2022 Beijing Games – the IOC finally released its much-anticipated 'Strategic Framework on Human Rights', linking it to the UN Guiding Principles on Business and Human Rights that tasks companies to respect human rights even when governments do not. (Human Rights Watch had been imploring the IOC to adopt such principles for years; in 2009, the group formally presented the idea to the Olympic Congress in Copenhagen.)[33] The IOC suggested it was open to 'amending the Olympic Charter to better articulate human rights responsibilities' and stated it was pondering the possibility of 'an independent third-party assessment on human rights to inform the selection of Future Hosts'. In addition, prospective Olympic hosts would be given a questionnaire on human rights.[34]

In October 2023, the IOC did amend the Olympic Charter to include some human-rights provisions. Two separate Fundamental Principles of Olympism now mention respect for 'internationally recognised human rights within the remit of the Olympic Movement'.[35] These changes subtly harden the false boundary between sports and politics. As scholar Wolfe put it,

'The word *remit* connotes that international sport has limits, and it is beyond the powers of the Olympic organisers to – for instance – sanction a Government that is aspiring to totalitarianism and that has launched a genocidal war against a neighbouring nation, buttressed by waves of terror and repression at home'.[36] So, the amendments create an alibi for IOC inaction in the face of human-rights abuses carried out by an Olympic host *outside the remit* of the Games.

Human Rights Watch's Worden noted that a 'framework assumes every country commits human rights abuses, because they do. But the framework only works if you're committed to identifying the abuses, remediating them, and being transparent about what bad things happened and what you did about them'. She added: 'The Olympics has a very serious problem in that it has adopted this framework that some of their bidders cannot possibly meet, and it may upend the entire process. It is worse to adopt the UN Guiding Principles and framework and then not uphold it.' She also questioned the value of a questionnaire:

Is a sheet of paper declaring human-rights problems adequate? No, it is not. You must do human-rights stakeholder assessments. You have to talk to actual human-rights experts. You can't just take a country's word for their human-rights problems, including the United States, the UK, or any country in the world.[37]

As human-rights scholar Barbara Keys puts it: when it comes to sports mega-events like the Olympics, 'moral claims are made in the spirit of incantation, like a liturgy based on faith, not facts'.[38] Evidence-driven oversight with teeth is required.

The IOC's strategic human-rights framework is part of a longer process. Since the 1990s, the IOC has worked alongside the UN on human-rights issues. In 2009 the UN assigned the IOC Permanent Observer status. Since 2011, the UN Human Rights Council has routinely advanced resolutions '[p]romoting human rights through sport and the Olympic ideal'.[39] Meanwhile, an upsurge of on-the-ground research by human-rights workers, academics, journalists, and grassroots activists has ratcheted up pressure on the IOC to solidify its commitment to human rights and, at the very least, obey its own charter. A clutch of human rights groups – groups like Human Rights Watch, Amnesty International, the Sport and Rights Alliance, Global Athlete, and the World Players Association – monitor the IOC's practices and rhetoric.

When Russia passed an anti-LGBTQ law ahead of the 2014 Sochi Olympics, many of these groups called out the IOC for failing to act. After all, the Olympic Charter in force at the time implicitly contained a principle protecting sexuality: 'Any form of discrimination ... on grounds of race, religion, politics, gender *or otherwise* is incompatible with belonging to the Olympic Movement.'[40]

Instead, even though the IOC had the power to act, it chose silence and then, after the Sochi Games, retooled its Charter to prohibit 'discrimination of any kind, such as race, colour, sex, *sexual orientation*, language, religion, political or other opinion, national or social origin, property, birth or other status'.[41]

Scholars have long argued that the IOC's rights rhetoric rings hollow. The IOC trumpets equality, freedom, and non-discrimination in its rhetoric, but foot-drags when it comes to meaningfully installing human-rights principles into its everyday practices. Historians Barbara Keys and Roland Burke assert that the elasticity of the term human rights makes it a go-to 'moral lingua franca' that provides 'a unique opportunity for theatrical virtue-signaling on a global scale'. They add that '[i]n a world of terrorist attacks, forever wars, and devastating civil conflicts, the UN and IOC have sought to buttress each other's faltering legitimacy with liturgical invocations of peace'.[42]

Human-rights groups have pressed the IOC to create systems of accountability. In January 2017 they convinced the IOC to revise its host-city contract to include human-rights principles, beginning with the 2024 Summer Games.[43] From that point onward, the host city, NOC, and local organizing committee are obligated to 'protect and respect human rights and ensure any violation of human rights is remedied in a manner consistent with international agreements, laws and regulations applicable in the Host Country and in a manner consistent with all internationally-recognised human rights standards and principles'.[44] By December 2018, the IOC initiated its own Human Rights Advisory Committee chaired by Prince Zeid Ra'ad Al Hussein of Jordan, the former UN High Commissioner for Human Rights. The committee slow-rolled the process until after the Beijing Olympics, something Worden of Human Rights Watch views as 'an active choice' and 'one of the darker moments of Olympic history'.[45]

Both Florence and Worden were sceptical of IOC President Thomas Bach's commitment to the cause. Under Bach, Florence said that the IOC has addressed human rights in 'very cosmetic ways', overseeing 'a pattern of policies that are just dragging on the process. Real change? Not really'. Florence said: 'The main legacy of Bach is to successfully look like he is doing something, but really just avoiding any real accountability from the IOC.'[46] Worden added:

> Bach could have put in place a framework to address the rampant abuse of children in sport, and instead rolled out a series of trainings for the presidents of NOCs and federations, which is completely inadequate because in many cases, the presidents are the ones either doing the abuse, or covering it up.

She insisted that:

> The adoption of a human-rights framework in theory could deal with the problem of sexual abuse in sport. When you think of the millions of children in the Olympic system, and the millions who never became Olympians because they were abused, that is a preventable human catastrophe that is a deep, historic responsibility that the IOC owns and that Thomas Bach as president owns.[47]

Moving forward, any IOC human rights policies must apply to all entities in the 'Olympic family', including, as Worden colourfully put it, 'all the corrupt kleptocrats at the head of the international sports federations' and NOCs as well.[48] The IOC needs to staff an enormous safeguarding department that can receive complaints of abuse and formulate concrete action plans. Florence suggested making the IOC's financial support for NOCs and IFs contingent on adhering to human-rights standards and compliance mechanisms while simultaneously establishing a fund for unpredictable impacts that require immediate remedy and accountability. She also said the IOC needs to be diversified in terms of leadership, members, management, and staff – European White men still disproportionately predominate.[49]

Athlete power

We are in the midst of a modern-day athlete empowerment era, with politically minded Olympians from numerous sports standing up and joining the fight for justice. Independent unions of athletes are forming across the globe to challenge injustices that are bricked into the Olympic system. Rob Koehler, the director general of Global Athlete, a transnational athlete-led group fighting for fairness in sport, said: 'We're seeing the rise of athlete advocacy that comes along with having independent representation. Athletes are realizing their space. They realize they have power, and they have the mechanism now through social media to tell their stories and to contribute to change.' When it comes to reforming the Olympics, Koehler asserted that '[e]qual-partnership collective bargaining and fixing the power imbalance' is the crux. 'That's the only way to do it.'[50] In the 21st century, athletes are demonstrating that they are up to the challenge. At the Tokyo 2020 Olympics, Raven Saunders, US silver medallist in the shot put, crossed her arms in the form of an X, explaining that the gesture represented 'the intersection of where all people who are oppressed meet' (see Figure 4.2). The IOC opted not to punish her.[51]

Many athletes would begin by eliminating the censorship currently imposed on them. This would entail amending the Olympic Charter, which openly

Figure 4.2: US shot-putter Raven Saunders expresses political dissent on the medal stand at the 2020 Tokyo Summer Olympics

curtails free speech. Although the Charter forbids discrimination based on politics and claims impatience for 'any political or commercial abuse of sport and athletes', it also includes Rule 50, which explicitly squelches political speech: 'No kind of demonstration or political, religious or racial propaganda is permitted in any Olympic sites, venues or other areas.'[52] This clashes with the UN's Universal Declaration of Human Rights, which asserts: 'Everyone has the right to freedom of opinion and expression; this right includes freedom to hold opinions without interference and to seek, receive and impart information and ideas through any media and regardless of frontiers.'[53] Rule 50 violates this bedrock principle. Under pressure from athletes and others, the IOC made slight adjustments to this rule ahead of the Tokyo 2020 Olympics, issuing guidelines that permitted Olympians to express their views 'on the field of play prior to the start of the competition' so long as they did not target specific individuals, countries, or groups and their actions were neither 'disruptive' nor an affront to anyone's dignity.[54]

This was a step in the right direction, but it is beyond time to abolish Rule 50 in its entirety. After all, as Nikki Dryden – who represented Canada at the 1992 and 1996 Olympics before becoming a human-rights lawyer – said: 'Once you get to the Olympics, you might have one fleeting moment in the light without anyone editing you. Olympians who choose to use that moment to shine attention on something of deep meaning to them should not be punished. In fact, they should be supported and celebrated.'[55]

Koehler of Global Athlete argued for an athlete-centred approach to the Olympics. 'Sport is really about athletes', he said, 'and if we are going to move forward into a better [sporting] environment, a better society, the athletes have to be equal partners'. Koehler insisted that this 'would help the IOC. It would help the athletes. And it would help the [Olympic] brand'. Equal partnership would pave a fairer path when it comes to anti-doping rules, safe-sport rules, and abuse in sport. 'It's all out of balance. It's a little bit like modern-day slavery. There's a lot of abuse', he said. Athletes lack basic rights and often 'have to accept whatever's thrown at them, and that's it'. He pointed to the 2022 Beijing Winter Olympics where 'athletes had no say' in the decision to hand the Games to China, 'yet they were the ones being criticized and asked why they weren't boycotting'. He emphasized, 'We need to focus on the IOC.'[56]

I believe we need to go further. It's time to abolish the IOC as it is currently constituted. For too long the band of out-of-touch power brokers running the Olympics have inhabited a world of five-star hotels, lavish perquisites, and, in some extreme instances, six-figure bribes. Meanwhile, athletes, who are the main attraction and moral core of the Games, are too often treated like second-class citizens on a five-ring doom loop. It's a double-standard – the best that money can buy for grifting princelings juxtaposed with the hardscrabble existence of too many hard-working Olympians – that the IOC has shown itself incapable of fixing. Great power requires great responsibility, and the almighty IOC has consistently failed to the live up to the responsibility it has to athletes and everyday residents in host cities. Given the IOC's demonstrated inability to work constructively with good-faith critics to foment change, this step, which may seem extreme to some, has now become necessary. Former and current athletes could step into this ethical vacuum to lead the Olympics boldly into the future alongside socially conscious, independent sports administrators and human-rights workers who specialize in sport.

Critical-thinking athletes – from independent groups like Global Athlete, the International Swimmers' Alliance, the Athletics Association in Track and Field, and the World Players Association – are capable of overseeing the Olympics and swerving the Games in an equitable direction. They would be an unequivocal improvement over the IOC's Athletes' Commission, the extant group of Olympians that operates under the umbrella of the IOC but that lacks the independence to speak truth to power. As Andrea Florence of the Sport and Rights Alliance put it, the Athletes' Commission is 'just a pawn for the IOC's policies'.[57] Koehler of Global Athlete asked: 'If you were an Athletes' Commission member representing athletes, why wouldn't you be fighting for athletes to gain a wage? Why would you have fought to not allow freedom of expression and Rule 50 at the Games?'[58]

Some Olympics mavens have already written off the current iteration of the IOC. Minky Worden of Human Rights Watch said that '[a]dapting the human-rights framework, however late, was important for the *future* leaders of the IOC. The current leaders do not have the capability to do it. Because of their footdragging approach, human-rights abusers haven't got the message that their time is up'. She added that '[a]thletes have the right to the IOC being their champion, and the IOC has, with very few exceptions, champion the abuser, and that's a very hard pattern to break'.[59]

Worden is onto something. IOC President Thomas Bach has consistently lashed out against good-faith critics rather than listen to them. 'We live in a world of mistrust against the establishment and we are considered to be part of this establishment', he inveighed in 2017. 'People are more and more thinking in silos of their own opinion. ... In a world of silos, they become aggressive of people who do not share their opinions.' Bach railed against such silo inhabitants who believe 'that they are in possession of the sole and only truth'. While Bach claimed that '[p]eople are not ready for a dialogue anymore', the reality is that the IOC needs to make a sincere and concerted effort to reach out to those both inside and outside the Olympic bubble whose lives are negatively affected by the Games.[60]

Abolishing today's IOC would help address thorny issues like doping in a more effective, athlete-centred way. Doping scholars April Henning and Paul Dimeo argue that the way doping is understood in the public sphere requires a serious rethink. 'There is no drug-free sport ... that is not enhanced in one way or another', they write, and the list of prohibitive substances is essentially an 'arbitrary line' based on the speculation and subjective assessment of a tiny group of anonymous scientists. They assert that we need to 'change the criteria on which decisions to prohibit a substance or method are based', shifting away from the 'spirit of sport' criterion and towards evidence-driven categories. They also argue for protecting athletes through clear-eyed education, fair testing, and proportionate sanctions. Athletes should get days off from being available for testing and the appeals process should be straightforward and efficient. And the entire system needs to be applied evenly across the globe.[61]

Koehler, who previously worked with the World Anti-Doping Agency (WADA), asked, 'Why shouldn't athletes have the ability to collectively bargain the [doping] rules?' He noted that '[a]thletes have everything to lose and everything to gain. This is all about them, and yet they don't have the collective approach to say, "These are the rules we want".' Moreover, 'WADA has no oversight', he said. In an authentic 'collective partnership, athletes would exert more control, like they do in professional leagues around the world where collective-bargaining power exists'.[62]

Democratize the Games

A third key area of reform involves democratizing the Olympic project at every turn. A democratic deficit twists through the history of the Olympics. Although Greece, home to the ancient Olympics, is known as a cradle of democracy, the founder of the modern

Games, Baron Pierre de Coubertin, was untroubled by criticism that the IOC was elitist and anti-democratic. In 1908, when confronted with allegations of the IOC's anti-democratic behaviour, he retorted pithily, 'We are not in the least concerned about it.' The Baron even doubled down on the IOC's manner of co-opting new members, stating, 'We are not elected. We are self-recruiting, and our terms of office are unlimited. Is there anything else that could irritate the public more?'[63]

Avery Brundage, the strong-willed and uncompromising president of the IOC between 1952 and 1972, followed suit, deriding the 'disadvantages of democracy'.[64] Brundage was an enthusiast for the White-only sport squads of apartheid South Africa and had an evident fondness for Franco's Spain, holding the IOC's 1965 congress in Madrid where the Generalissimo provided the opening speech. Brundage followed Franco with fulsome praise for the dictator's firm grasp of the principles of amateurism.[65] Brundage's eventual successor, Juan Antonio Samaranch, who helmed the IOC from 1980 to 2001, was a former Franco functionary who took on a number of leadership roles for the Falangists – from fascist parliamentarian to sports minister – over the course of nearly four decades of service. Samaranch regarded himself as 'one hundred per cent Francoist' up to the dictator's death.[66]

One way to inject more democracy into the Olympic process would be to require every Olympic bid to include a public referendum where everyday people in the Olympic city could weigh in. Given that taxpayer money is typically shovelled into the Olympics and that many of those taxpaying city dwellers will not be able to afford a ticket to the Games, giving them a chance to have a say is a necessary, if basic, courtesy. Olympic boosters often correctly exclaim what a big deal it is to host the Games, so allowing locals to voice their opinion on something that will affect their lives is common sense.

When the Olympics have experienced outbursts of democracy during the bid process – in the form of public plebiscites or referenda – people have overwhelmingly rejected the Games. Between 2013 and 2018, Olympic bids lost a whopping eight public votes. Citizens in Hamburg, Innsbruck, Kraków, Munich, Sion (Switzerland), and Vienna voted against hosting the Olympics. Voters in Graubünden, Switzerland rejected the Games twice. After Oslo's bid was approved in a public referendum, the bid was kneecapped by public pressure demanding a rethink.[67] One must go all the way back to 2003 – when 64 per cent of Vancouver voters supported the city's Olympic bid in a plebiscite – to find a successful Olympic vote where the city went on to land the Games.[68] In doing so, pro-Olympics boosters in Vancouver spent $700,000 persuading the public – 140 times more than the 'no' side – notes Olympics critic Helen Jefferson Lenskyj.[69]

Partly in response to numerous cities saying no to the Games, the IOC, under the direction of President Thomas Bach, revamped the bid process, but not in a democratic direction. As noted earlier, the

IOC conceived two Future Host Commissions for the Summer and Winter Olympics comprised of a maximum of ten members.[70] This essentially relegates the rest of the IOC to rubber-stamp status. The new bid process is actually *less democratic*, replete with 'confidential discussions' behind closed doors.[71] As noted in the Introduction, IOC power broker John Coates, the longtime head of the Australian Olympic Committee, chaired the working group that recommended the Future Host Commissions.[72] Then, using this new process, the IOC handed the 2032 Summer Olympics to Brisbane despite very little public discussion of the bid, let alone a referendum.[73] So, recent changes to the Olympic bidding process actually undercut democracy, affording everyday people a diminished chance to participate.

In May 2021, when public opinion in Japan pivoted against staging the Tokyo Olympics as COVID-19 cases rose in Japan, one IOC spokesperson uttered what could be the nine most terrifying words in the Olympic lexicon: 'We listen but won't be guided by public opinion.'[74] If the Olympics are to live up to their own stated ideals, this needs to change. When in doubt, democratize it out. In addition to installing public referenda as a mandatory part of every Olympic bid, the IOC's own voting practices require more transparency. The IOC should make public all votes for future Olympic host cities, thereby following the lead of FIFA, the world's governing body for soccer.

None of these reforms will be easy. The Olympics are a powerful goliath – replete with entrenched norms and ambitious power brokers – with leaders who have shown a dogged determination to maintain the money-flow status quo. The IOC is a refined, effective virtue-projection apparatus. And yet, if bold change does not come now, then when?

Continuous struggle

The Olympics are a skeleton key that can unlock understanding of wider trends in society. This book has examined two criss-crossing societal trajectories in tension:

1. the rise of the Olympics as a massive cultural and economic force and the emergence of endemic downsides that have galvanized significant criticism of the Games; and
2. the fortification of the International Olympic Committee's power as it firmly fused itself to television broadcasters and corporate sponsors and a surge in anti-Olympics activism around the globe that both reflects and refracts the fact that fewer and fewer cities are game to host the Games.

In a way, the COVID-19 virus was tantamount to a massive injection of dye – as used in an imaging exam – into the Olympics in that it revealed in glaring contrast the imperfections not only in the Tokyo 2020 and Beijing 2022 Olympics, but within the Olympic body more generally. The Tokyo Olympics threw a spotlight on the stark reality that the Games are not so much broken as they are fixed – fixed in favour of the powerful people and entities that run the mega-event. And yet, because of the enormous popularity of the Games, because of the remarkable athletes whose feats still rivet us to our seats, because of the communities negatively affected by the five-ring juggernaut who deserve better, the Olympics must be adjusted to align word and deed and to imbue the whole affair with real-deal justice from top to bottom. If not, then the IOC, as currently constituted, must go. If that's impossible, then the widespread activist chant 'NOlympics Anywhere' may well be the next best path (see Figure 4.3).

Figure 4.3: Activists gather in Tokyo, July 2019

Activists from around the world gather behind a banner reading 'NOlympics Anywhere!' that was created by protesters from Los Angeles.

Sport arrives with an implicit promise to each and every athlete that their sporting journey will offer precious life lessons, enhance their lives with lifelong relationships, and provide the joy of movement. As geographer Yi-Fu Tuan wrote, '[f]or ... athletes life is joyous in its vitality, and vitality is motion during which time is forgotten, space becomes freedom, self and world unite'.[75] And yet, too often, the structure of elite-level sport nestled inside the Olympics robs athletes of these gems and pleasures. Therefore, it is imperative to demand that the IOC lives up to its stated commitment to 'social responsibility and respect for universal fundamental ethical principles'.[76]

Much has changed since Baron Pierre de Coubertin was the key chemist concocting the alchemy of Olympic ideology. The Olympic Games have expanded massively into a popular force in society with symbology that is instantly recognizable across the globe. One estimate found that 95 per cent of the global population recognized the Olympic rings.[77] Such social power implicitly brings great responsibility. On this front, the IOC has much room for improvement.

Martin Luther King Jr. insisted that '[c]hange does not roll in on the wheels of inevitability, but comes through continuous struggle'.[78] To achieve meaningful social change that would fix the inequities that are bricked into the Olympics, people who care about the Games must collectively press ahead with vim and compassion, with zest and grit, with historical knowledge and forward-thinking ingenuity, with open-mindedness and a commitment to justice.

NOTES

Introduction

[1]   David Wharton, 'L.A. City Council Endorses 2028 Olympics Bid, Accepting Responsibility for Any Cost Overruns', *Los Angeles Times*, 11 August 2017; Jules Boykoff, *NOlympians: Inside the Fight Against Capitalist Mega-Sports in Los Angeles, Tokyo, and Beyond* (Fernwood Publishing, 2020), pp 39–40.

[2]   Eileen Rivers, 'Noah Says Olympics Are Getting "Desperate" in Best of Late Night', *USA Today*, 29 March 2019.

[3]   Motoko Rich and Hikari Hida, 'As Covid Cases Hit Record High in Tokyo, Can the Olympic Bubble Hold?', *New York Times*, 29 July 2021; Jules Boykoff, 'Tokyo Is Learning that the Only Force Stronger than a Pandemic Is the Olympics', *Washington Post*, 27 May 2021.

[4]   Ed Aarons and Romain Molina, '"Uniquely Qualified": John Coates Drafted Letter of Praise for Himself to Brisbane Olympics Organizers', *Guardian*, 30 April 2022.

[5]   Thomas Bach, 'The Olympics Are about Unity and Diversity, Not Politics and Profit. Boycotts Don't Work', *Guardian*, 23 October 2020.

[6]   Brad Adgate, 'TV Ratings for Beijing Winter Olympics Was an All-Time Low; For Streaming It Was an All-Time High', *Forbes*, 23 February 2022.

[7]   In the 2017–2020/21 cycle, broadcaster rights accounted for 61 per cent of IOC revenue. For the 2013–2016 cycle, it was 73 per cent. International Olympic Committee, 'Annual Report 2021: Faster, Higher, Stronger – Together', Lausanne, Switzerland, 2022, p 173; International Olympic Committee, '2020 Annual Report: Credibility, Sustainability, Youth', Lausanne, Switzerland, 2021, p 147.

[8]   Ed Aarons and Romain Molina, 'Sydney Olympics Were Bought "To a Large Extent," Said Australian Official John Coates', *Guardian*, 1 May 2022.

9   Jules Boykoff, 'The Olympic Are Political: The IOC Ban Denies Reality – And Athletes Their Voice', *NBC News Think*, 16 January 2020.

10   Geoff Berkeley, 'Bach and Coates Underline Russia-Belarus Stance as AOC Donates to Ukraine Solidarity Fund', *Inside the Games*, 30 April 2022; Sammy Mncwabe, 'Russian and Belarusian Athlete Participation "Works" Despite War, Says IOC President Thomas Bach', *CNN*, 28 March 2023.

11   Philip Barker, 'Ukrainian President Zelenskyy Tells Bach During Kyiv Meeting that Russia Has No Place in World Sport', *Inside the Games*, 3 July 2022.

12   See: https://twitter.com/iocmedia/status/1546564570944241664?s=20&t=P0RAyJNEkekrUS-LRe2Z1Q

13   International Olympic Committee, 'Putting Athletes First', *Olympic Review* (2017), pp 36–42.

14   Chen Chen, 'Naming the Ghost of Capitalism in Sport Management', *European Sport Management Quarterly* 22 (2022), pp 663–84.

Chapter 1

1   Kristina Andělová, 'Czechoslovak Generational Experience of 1968: The Intellectual History Perspective', *East European Politics and Societies and Cultures* 33 (2019), pp 881–98.

2   Thomas J. Hamilton, 'Czechoslovak Team Going to Olympics as Difficulties of Occupation Ease', *New York Times*, 15 September 1968, p S9.

3   Allen Guttmann, *The Olympics: A History of the Modern Games* (2nd edition) (University of Illinois Press, 2002 [1992]).

4   Vitor S. Tardelli, Tathiana R. Parmigiano, João M. Castaldelli-Maia, and Thiago M. Fidalgo, 'Pressure Is Not a Privilege: What We Can Learn from Simone Biles', *Brazilian Journal of Psychiatry* 43 (2021), pp 460–1.

5   Emily Giambalvo, 'Simone Biles Withdraws from Vault and Uneven Bars Finals', *Washington Post*, 30 July 2021.

6   Michael D. Shear, '"This Is America": Biden Honors 17 with Presidential Medal of Freedom', *New York Times*, 7 July 2022.

7   Pierre de Coubertin, *Olympism: Selected Writings*, Norbert Müller (ed) (International Olympic Committee, 2000), p 548.

8   Coubertin, *Olympism*, p 228, p 202.

9   Coubertin, *Olympism*, p 580, emphasis in original.

10   Coubertin, *Olympism*, p 580, emphasis in original.

11   Heather L. Reid, 'Olympism: A Philosophy of Sport?', in McNamee and Morgan (eds) *Routledge Handbook of the Philosophy of Sport* (Routledge, 2015), p 374.

12   Coubertin, *Olympism*, p 582, p 583, emphasis in original.

13   International Olympic Committee, 'Gender Equality and Youth at the Heart of the Paris 2024 Olympic Sports Program', 7 December 2020.

14   International Olympic Committee, *Olympic Charter*, 8 August 2021, p 8.

15   International Olympic Committee, *Olympic Charter*, p 8.

16   Jean-Loup Chappelet and Brenda Kübler-Mabbott, *The International Olympic Committee and the Olympic System: The Governance of World Sport* (Routledge, 2008); Jean-Loup Chappelet, 'The Governance of the Olympic System: From One to Many Stakeholders', *Journal of Global Sport Management* (2021), pp 1–18.

17   International Olympic Committee, *Olympic Charter*, pp 60–4.

18   Scott Jedlicka, 'Sport Governance as Global Governance: Theoretical Perspectives on Sport in the International System', *International Journal of Sport Policy and Politics* 10 (2018), pp 287–304; Chappelet and Kübler-Mabbott, *The International Olympic Committee and the Olympic System*, pp 59–77.

19   International Olympic Committee, *Olympic Charter*, pp 56–7, pp 86–7.

20   Chappelet, 'The Governance of the Olympic System', p 4.

21   Chappelet, 'The Governance of the Olympic System', p 4; Chappelet and Kübler-Mabbott, *The International Olympic Committee and the Olympic System*, pp 90–3.

22   International Olympic Committee, *Olympic Charter*, pp 75–6.

23   Michael Pavitt, 'Tokyo 2020 Organising Committee to Dissolve and Confirm Final Games Cost in June', *Inside the Games*, 24 March 2022.

24   Chappelet, 'The Governance of the Olympic System', p 5.

25   International Olympic Committee, *Olympic Charter*, p 63, p 64. Also see: Chappelet and Kübler-Mabbott, *The International Olympic Committee and the Olympic System*; Chappelet, 'The Governance of the Olympic System'.

26   International Olympic Committee, 'Annual Report 2021: Faster, Higher, Stronger – Together', 2022, p 173.

27   Robert K. Barney, Stephen R. Wenn, and Scott G. Martyn, *Selling the Five Rings: The International Olympic Committee and the*

Rise of Olympic Commercialism (University of Utah Press, 2004), pp 54–5, p 75.

28 Stephen R. Wenn, 'An Olympian Squabble: The Distribution of Olympic Television Revenue, 1960–1966', *Olympika: The International Journal of Olympic Studies* 3 (1994), p 47.

29 Jim Reindel, 'IOC Posts $7.6 Billion in Revenue Over the Expanded Olympic Cycle', *Around the Rings*, 23 May 2022.

30 John Horne and Garry Whannel, *Understanding the Olympics* (Routledge, 2012), p 60.

31 Jules Boykoff, *Power Games: A Political History of the Olympics* (Verso, 2016), pp 130–6.

32 Yuri Kageyama and Stephen Wade, 'Tokyo Games Sponsors Pay $3.3 Billion, But More Still Needed', *Associated Press*, 11 December 2020.

33 International Olympic Committee, 'Annual Report 2020: Credibility, Sustainability, Youth', 2021, p 155; International Olympic Committee, 'Annual Report 2021', p 181.

34 International Olympic Committee, 'The Olympic Movement, the IOC, and the Olympic Games' (Olympic Studies Centre, 15 December 2021), p 8.

35 Chappelet and Kübler-Mabbott, *The International Olympic Committee and the Olympic System*, p 19.

36 John J. MacAloon, *This Great Symbol: Pierre de Coubertin and the Origins of the Modern Olympics* (Routledge, 2008), p 202.

37 International Olympic Committee, 'Future Host Commissions: Terms of Reference', 3 October 2019, pp 1–13.

38 Jean-Loup Chappelet, 'Switzerland's Century-Long Rise as the Hub of Global Sport Administration', *The International Journal of the History of Sport* 38 (2021), p 580, p 583.

39 Aaron Gordon, 'IOC to Rio 2016: We Will Not Help Pay Your Olympic Debt', *Vice*, 10 July 2017.

40 Chappelet, 'Switzerland's Century-Long Rise as the Hub of Global Sport Administration', pp 569–90.

41 Horne and Whannel, *Understanding the Olympics*, p 28.

42 See: https://olympics.com/ioc/members

43 International Olympic Committee, 'Annual Report 2021', p 121.

44 International Olympic Committee, 'The Olympic Movement, the IOC, and the Olympic Games', p 9.

45 'Olympic Bribery Scandal Chronology', *Associated Press*, 3 August 1999.

46   George J. Mitchell, Kenneth Duberstein, Donald Fehr, Roberta Cooper Ramo, and Jeffrey G. Benz, 'Report of the Special Bid Oversight Commission', US Senate, 1 March 1999, p 9.

47   Stephen Wenn, Robert Barney, and Scott Martyn, *Tarnished Rings: The International Olympic Committee and the Salt Lake City Bid Scandal* (Syracuse University Press, 2011), pp 22–3, p 47; 'Olympic Bribery Scandal Chronology', *Associated Press*, 3 August 1999.

48   Chappelet and Kübler-Mabbott, *The International Olympic Committee and the Olympic System*, pp 17–18.

49   Lorenzo Casini, 'The Making of a *Lex Sportiva* by the Court of Arbitration for Sport', *German Law Journal* 12 (2011), pp 1317–40.

50   Helen Lenskyj, 'Sport Exceptionalism and the Court of Arbitration for Sport', *Journal of Criminological Research, Policy, and Practice* 4 (2018), pp 5–17.

51   Antoine Duval, 'Lost in Translation? The European Convention on Human Rights at the Court of Arbitration for Sport', *The International Sports Law Journal* (2022), pp 1–20.

52   Thomas M. Hunt, *Drug Games: The International Olympic Committee and the Politics of Doping* (University of Texas Press, 2011).

53   International Olympic Committee, 'Annual Report 2021', p 129.

54   International Olympic Committee, 'Future Host Commissions: Terms of Reference', p 13.

55   International Olympic Committee, 'Putting Athletes First', *Olympic Review* (2017), pp 36–42.

56   I do not analyse the Paralympics in this book, although there are some overlaps with the Olympics, as with fiscal contributions from the IOC. On one hand, the Paralympics are essentially a sporty barnacle on the Olympic ship in that they follow the Olympics wherever they dock. On the other hand, they emerged later than the Olympics, are overseen by a separate group called the International Paralympic Committee, and enjoy substantially less economic power (thus making them reliant on the Olympics and the IOC for funding and support). The roots of the Paralympics reach back to the 1940s, when Ludwig Guttmann started using sports as part of the rehabilitation process for people who had suffered spinal-cord injuries. His goal was twofold: the social reintegration of people with disabilities and the wider cultural project of changing societal perceptions about disability. After staging a number of 'Stoke Mandeville Games' in England between

1948 and 1959 – featuring sports like archery and swimming – the first Paralympics to debut in parallel with the Olympics took place in 1960 in Rome. Beginning in 1988, each Summer Paralympic Games has commenced around two weeks after the Olympics. The Paralympics have a distinct field of scholarship. See: Ian Brittain, *The Paralympic Games Explained* (2nd edition) (Routledge, 2016); Simon Darcy, Stephen Frawley, and Daryl Adair (eds) *Managing the Paralympics* (Palgrave Macmillan, 2017); David Howe, *The Cultural Politics of the Paralympic Movement: Through an Anthropological Lens* (Routledge, 2008).

[57]   International Olympic Committee, 'Annual Report 2021', p 174.
[58]   Jens Weinreich, 'How Federations Share the Revenues from the Olympic Games', *Play the Game*, 3 April 2020.
[59]   Colby Itkowitz, 'The Hardest Part about Making the Olympics for these Americans? Affording It', *Washington Post*, 6 July 2016.
[60]   Cheri Bradish, Rob Koehler, and Andrew Bailey, 'Olympic Commercialization and Player Compensation: A Review of Olympic Financial Reports', The Ted Rogers School of Management in Partnership with Global Athlete, 6 December 2019, pp 1–20. Until 2022, Toronto Metropolitan University was called Ryerson University.

Chapter 2

[1]   Angelo Bolanaki, 'The Olympic Flag: Its History and Use', *Bulletin du Comité International Olympique* 27 (June 1951), pp 42–3. In 2021, the IOC officially adapted the motto to read 'Citius, Altius, Fortius – Communiter' ('Faster, Higher, Stronger – Together') to capture the Games' spirit of unity.
[2]   'Baron Coubertin's Heart Buried in Olympia Stadium', *New York Times*, 27 March 1938, p 29.
[3]   Pierre de Coubertin, 'The Olympic Games of 1896', *The Century Magazine* 53 (November 1896), p 53.
[4]   Pierre de Coubertin, *Olympism: Selected Writings*, Norbert Müller (ed) (International Olympic Committee, 2000), p 303.
[5]   Coubertin, 'The Olympic Games of 1896', p 53.
[6]   Cited in Bruce Kidd, 'The Aspirations of Olympism: A Framework for Considering the Athlete's Experience in the Olympic Movement at the Close of the Twentieth Century' (Centre d'Estudis Olímpics UAB, 2000), p 13.
[7]   Coubertin, *Olympism*, p 147.
[8]   Coubertin, *Olympism*, pp 580–81, emphasis in original.

9   John J. MacAloon, *This Great Symbol: Pierre de Coubertin and the Origins of the Modern Olympics* (Routledge, 2008), p 6.

10 David C. Young, *A Brief History of the Olympics* (Blackwell Publishing, 2004), p 94.

11 Alfred E. Senn, *Power, Politics, and the Olympic Games* (Human Kinetics, 1999), pp 9–10.

12 Jean Durry, '"Hohrod and Eschbach": A Mystery Finally Solved', *Olympic Review* 26 (April–May 2000), pp 26–8.

13 Coubertin, 'The Olympic Games of 1896', p 50.

14 Quoted in Ljubodrag Simonović, *Philosophy of Olympism* (Stručna Knjiga, 2004), p 40.

15 Coubertin, *Olympism*, p 498.

16 Coubertin, *Olympism*, p 498.

17 Coubertin, *Olympism*, p 315.

18 Coubertin, *Olympism*, p 713.

19 Quoted in Kevin B. Wamsley and Guy Schultz, 'Rogues and Bedfellows: The IOC and the Incorporation of the FSFI', Western Ontario University, *Fifth International Symposium for Olympic Research* (2000), p 113.

20 Coubertin, *Olympism*, p 713.

21 Coubertin, *Olympism*, p 746.

22 Jaime Schultz, *Women's Sports: What Everyone Needs to Know* (Oxford University Press, 2018), p 16.

23 Rita Amaral Nunes, 'Women Athletes in the Olympic Games', *Journal of Human Sport and Exercise* 14 (2019), pp 676–7.

24 David Goldblatt, *The Games: A Global History of the Olympics* (W.W. Norton & Company, 2016), p 42.

25 Goldblatt, *The Games*, p 44; Coubertin, *Olympism*, p 324; Christopher R. Hill, *Olympic Politics* (2nd edition) (Manchester University Press, 1996), p 27.

26 David C. Young, *The Modern Olympics: A Struggle for Revival* (Johns Hopkins University Press, 1996), pp 116–26; Richard Mandell, *The First Modern Olympics* (University of California Press, 1976), p 97, p 100.

27 Goldblatt, *The Games*, p 48, p 47.

28 David Miller, *The Official History of the Olympic Games and the IOC: Athens to London 1894 to 2012* (Mainstream Publishing Company, 2012), pp 38–42.

29 David Clay Large, *Nazi Games: The Olympics of 1936* (W.W. Norton & Company, 2007), p 198.

30   Pierre de Coubertin, T.J. Philemon, N.G. Politis, and Charalambos Anninos, *The Olympic Games, B.C. 776 –A.D. 1896* (H. Grevel and Co., 1897), p 107.

31   Coubertin, *Olympism*, p 332.

32   Coubertin, 'The Olympic Games of 1896', p 39.

33   Coubertin, *Olympism*, p 394.

34   Allen Guttmann, *The Olympics: A History of the Modern Games* (2nd edition) (University of Illinois Press, 2002 [1992]), pp 22–4; Senn, *Power, Politics, and the Olympic Games*, p 25.

35   Miller, *The Official History of the Olympic Games and the IOC*, pp 54–6.

36   James E. Sullivan, 'Anthropology Days at the Stadium', in Sullivan (ed) *Spalding's Official Athletic Almanac for 1905* (American Sports Publishing, 1905), p 249.

37   Nancy J. Parezo, 'A "Special Olympics": Testing Racial Strength and Endurance at the 1904 Louisiana Purchase Exhibition', in Brownell (ed) *The 1904 Anthropology Days and Olympic Games: Sport, Race, and American Imperialism* (University of Nebraska Press, 2008), p 60.

38   Coubertin, *Olympism*, p 695, p 407.

39   Miller, *The Official History of the Olympic Games and the IOC*, p 54.

40   Miller, *The Official History of the Olympic Games and the IOC*, p 57.

41   Karl Lennartz, 'The 2nd International Olympic Games in Athens 1906', *Journal of Olympic History* 10 (2002), pp 10–27; Mark Quinn, *The King of Spring: The Life and Times of Peter O'Connor* (The Liffey Press, 2004), p 172.

42   Quinn, *The King of Spring*, p 172.

43   Quinn, *The King of Spring*, p 176; David Guiney, 'The Olympic Council of Ireland', *Citius, Altius, Fortius* 4 (1996), pp 31–3.

44   Personal interview, 23 June 2014.

45   Guiney, 'The Olympic Council of Ireland', p 33; Quinn, *The King of Spring*, pp 184–5.

46   Quinn, *The King of Spring*, p 184.

47   Stephen Halliday, 'London's Olympics, 1908', *History Today* 58 (April 2008), https://www.historytoday.com/archive/londons-olympics-1908

48   Halliday, 'London's Olympics, 1908'; Guttmann, *The Olympics*, p 29.

49   Goldblatt, *The Games*, p 77.

50 Halliday, 'London's Olympics, 1908'.
51 'Drastic Rules for American Oarsmen', *New York Times*, 6 September 1907, p 7.
52 Stephanie Daniels and Anita Tedder, *'A Proper Spectacle': Women Olympians 1900–1936* (Walla Walla Press, 2000), p 27.
53 Robert Reising, 'Jim Thorpe: Multi-Cultural Hero', *The Indian Historian* 3 (1974), pp 14–16.
54 Erik Bergvall and Swedish Olympic Committee, 'The Official Report of the Olympic Games of Stockholm 1912', pp 410–11.
55 Jack McCallum, 'The Regilding of a Legend', *Sports Illustrated*, 25 October 1982.
56 International Olympic Committee, 'IOC to Display the Name of Jim Thorpe as Sole Stockholm 1912 Pentathlon and Decathlon Gold Medallist', 15 July 2022.
57 Coubertin, *Olympism*, p 598.
58 Coubertin, *Olympism*, p 645, p 457.
59 Young, *The Modern Olympics*, p 41.
60 Coubertin, *Olympism*, p 465.
61 Guttmann, *The Olympics*, p 38; Coubertin, *Olympism*, p 472.
62 Coubertin, *Olympism*, p 486; Senn, *Power, Politics, and the Olympic Games*, pp 39–40.
63 International Olympic Committee, 'Factsheet: Women in the Olympic Movement', May 2014.
64 Wamsley and Schultz, 'Rogues and Bedfellows', pp 113–18; Carly Adams, 'Fighting for Acceptance: Sigfrid Edstrom and Avery Brundage: Their Efforts to Shape and Control Women's Participation in the Olympic Games', *Sixth International Symposium for Olympic Research* (2002), pp 143–8; Mary H. Leigh and Thérèse M. Bonin, 'The Pioneering Role of Madame Alice Milliat and the FSFI in Establishing International Track and Field Competition for Women', *Journal of Sport History* 4 (1977), pp 72–83.
65 Uriel Simri, *Women at the Olympic Games* (Wingate Monograph Series, 1979); Wamsley and Schultz, 'Rogues and Bedfellows'; Adams, 'Fighting for Acceptance'; Leigh and Bonin, 'The Pioneering Role of Madame Alice Milliat'.
66 James Riordan, 'The Worker Sports Movement', in Riordan and Krüger (eds) *The International Politics of Sport in the Twentieth Century* (E&FN SPON, 1999), pp 105–17.
67 Robert F. Wheeler, 'Organized Sport and Organized Labour: The Workers' Sport Movement', *Journal of Contemporary History* 13 (1978), p 200; Arnd Krüger, 'The German Way of Worker Sport',

in Krüger and Riordan (eds) *The Story of Worker Sport* (Human Kinetics, 1996), p 17.

68 Wheeler, 'Organized Sport and Organized Labour', p 201; Riordan, 'The Worker Sports Movement', pp 111–12.

69 '$1,000,000 Stadium Ready in Vienna', *New York Times*, 19 July 1931, p E4.

70 Wheeler, 'Organized Sport and Organized Labour', p 202; Riordan, 'The Worker Sport Movement', p 113.

71 Jules Boykoff, *The 1936 Berlin Olympics: Race, Power, and Sportswashing* (Common Ground Publishing, 2023).

72 Richard Mandell, *The Nazi Olympics* (University of Illinois Press, 1987), p 130.

73 Quoted in Richard Menkins and Harold Troper, *More Than Just Games: Canada and the 1936 Olympics* (University of Toronto Press, 2015), p 190.

74 Mandell, *The Nazi Olympics*, pp 148–50; Large, *Nazi Games*, pp 194–5.

75 Jules Boykoff, 'Toward a Theory of Sportswashing: Mega-Events, Soft Power, and Political Conflict', *Sociology of Sport Journal* 39 (2022), pp 342–51.

76 Organizing Committee for the XI Olympiad Berlin 1936, 'XIth Olympic Games Berlin, 1936: Official Report, Volume I' (Wilhelm Limpert, 1936), p 560, p 547.

77 Coubertin, *Olympism*, p 521.

78 Guy Walters, *Berlin Games: How the Nazis Stole the Olympic Dream* (Harper Perennial, 2006), pp 143–6; Mario Kessler, 'Only Nazi Games? Berlin 1936: The Olympic Games between Sports and Politics', *Socialism and Democracy* 25 (2011), pp 125–43.

79 Jeremy Schaap, *Triumph: The Untold Story of Jesse Owens and Hitler's Olympics* (Houghton Mifflin Company, 2007), p 165.

80 David K. Wiggins, *Glory Bound: Black Athletes in White America* (Syracuse University Press, 1997), p 73.

81 Miller, *The Official History of the Olympic Games and the IOC*, pp 133–4.

82 Guttmann, *The Olympics*, p 97.

83 Goldblatt, *The Games*, pp 216–17.

84 Harrison Salisbury, 'Russians Hail Olympic "Victory" But Fail to Substantiate Claim', *New York Times*, 5 August 1952, p 23.

85 Boykoff, *Power Games*, pp 81–2; Thomas M. Hunt, *Drug Games: The International Olympic Committee and the Politics of Doping* (University of Texas Press, 2011), p 7.

86   Xu Guoqi, *Olympic Dreams: China and Sports, 1895–2008* (Harvard University Press, 2008), pp 77–83; Hill, *Olympic Politics*, pp 44–6.

87   Allison Danzig, 'Brundage Is Chosen Over Briton as Head of International Olympic Committee', *New York Times*, 17 July 1952, p 28

88   Miller, *The Official History of the Olympic Games and the IOC*, p 144.

89   Avery Brundage, 'Memorandum', 18 March 1950, Avery Brundage Collection (ABC), Box 10, Reel 6, International Centre for Olympic Studies (ICOS), London, Ontario.

90   Avery Brundage, 'Speech in Munich', nd, 4, ABC, Box 249, Reel 144, ICOS.

91   Avery Brundage, 'Address at the 67th Solemn Opening Session, Mexico City, Mexico', 7 October 1968, 9, ABC, Box 246, Reel 143, ICOS.

92   Avery Brundage, 'Untitled', in folder 'Avery Brundage Book – Politics U.S.A', ABC, Box 243, Reel 141, ICOS.

93   Avery Brundage, 'Politics', in file 'Notes on Art, Politics, Sports, 1968–1970', ABC, Box 246, Reel 143, ICOS.

94   Avery Brundage, 'Politics', in folder 'Memos, Notes, etc. by Avery Brundage on Sports, Art, Politics, 1952–1958', ABC, Box 245, Reel 142, ICOS.

95   'Olympics Rebuff South Africans', *New York Times*, 28 January 1964, p 36.

96   'Boycotting South Africa', *Time*, 8 March 1968, p 88.

97   Harry Edwards, *The Revolt of the Black Athlete* (The Free Press, 1969), pp 58–9.

98   John Carlos and Dave Zirin, *The John Carlos Story: The Sports Moment that Changed the World* (Haymarket Books, 2011); Tommie Smith with David Steele, *Silent Gesture: The Autobiography of Tommie Smith* (Temple University Press, 2007).

99   'Statement of the US Olympic Committee', 17 October 1968, ABC, Box 179, Reel 103, ICOS.

100   Wyomia Tyus and Elizabeth Terzakis, *Tigerbelle: The Wyomia Tyus Story* (Akashic Books, 2018), p 183.

101   Douglas Hartmann, *Race, Culture, and the Revolt of the Black Athlete: The 1968 Olympic Protests and their Aftermath* (University of Chicago Press, 2003); David K. Wiggins, 'Vince Matthews, Wayne Collett, and the Forgotten Disruption in

Munich', *The Journal of African American History* 106 (2021), pp 278–303.

102 Vincent Matthews with Neil Amdur, *My Race Be Won* (Charterhouse, 1974), p 340.

103 Matthews with Amdur, *My Race Be Won*, p 356.

104 Neil Amdur, 'Matthews and Collett Banned from Olympics', *New York Times*, 9 September 1972, p 17.

105 International Olympic Committee, 'Olympic Rules 1975 (Provisional Edition)', 1975, p 35, https://stillmed.olympic.org/ Documents/Olympic%20Charter/Olympic_Charter_through_ time/1975-Olympic_Charter-Olympic_Rules.pdf

106 Eddie Pells, '50 Years Later, Sprinter Matthews Welcomed Back to Olympics', *Associated Press*, 12 December 2022.

107 Hill, *Olympic Politics*, p 36.

108 Adam Berg, *The Olympics That Never Happened: Denver '76 and the Politics of Growth* (University of Texas Press, 2023).

109 'Montreal Olympics 1976: "Self-financing?"' *CBC*, 29 January 1973.

110 Robert Trumbull, 'Olympic Advertising Is Planned', *New York Times*, 15 October 1974, p 59.

111 Robert Trumbull, 'High Costs of Games Studied', *New York Times*, 28 August 1976, p 35.

112 Robert Lindsey, '84 Olympics Facing Financing Struggle', *New York Times*, 19 August 1979, p 18; '1984 Olympics to Rely on Private Enterprise', *New York Times*, 6 December 1981, p 31; 'Los Angeles Appears Ready for Withdrawal of 1984 Olympics Bid', *New York Times*, 19 July 1978, p 19.

113 Neil Amdur, 'Los Angeles Assured of Games', *New York Times*, 11 February 1979, p S1.

114 Kenneth Reich, *Making It Happen: Peter Ueberroth and the 1984 Olympics* (Capra Press, 1986), p 12.

115 Peter Ueberroth, with Richard Levin and Amy Quinn, *Made in America: His Own Story* (William Morrow and Company, Inc., 1985).

116 Richard Perelman, *Olympic Retrospective: The Games of Los Angeles* (Los Angeles Olympic Organizing Committee, 1985), pp 94–107.

117 Alan Tomlinson, 'The Disneyfication of the Olympics: Theme Parks and Freak-Shows of the Body', in Bale and Krogh Christensen (eds) *Post-Olympism? Questioning Sport in the Twenty-first Century* (Berg Publishers, 2004), pp 147–63.

118   'Los Angeles Olympic Organizing Committee, Official Report of
      the Games of the XXIIIrd Olympiad Los Angeles, 1984', Volume 1,
      1985, p 26. Some gauged the surplus slightly higher: $232 million.
      See Perelman, *Olympic Retrospective*, p 119.

119   Pamela G. Hollie, 'Big Mac's Olympic Giveaway', *New York
      Times*, 10 August 1984.

120   Miller, *The Official History of the Olympic Games and the IOC*,
      p 250.

121   Goldblatt, *The Games*, p 329.

122   Sabine M'Bodj, 'ISL Marketing AG', *Olympic Review* 25 (1995),
      p 28.

123   International Olympic Committee, 'Annual Report 2021: Faster,
      Higher, Stronger – Together', 2022, p 173.

124   Robert K. Barney, Stephen R. Wenn, and Scott G. Martyn, *Selling
      the Five Rings: The International Olympic Committee and the
      Rise of Olympic Commercialism* (University of Utah Press, 2004),
      p 163.

125   International Olympic Committee, 'Annual Report 2021', p 173.

126   Kim Tong-Hyung, 'Evictees from S Korea's First Olympics Recall
      Harsh Clearings', Associated Press, 8 March 2018.

127   Hunt, *Drug Games*, pp 80–3.

128   Barcelona Holding Olímpic S.A., 'Los Juegos Olímpicos Como
      Generadores de Inversión (1986–1992)', Barcelona, 1992, p 7.

129   Ferran Brunet, 'Analysis of the Economic Impact of the Olympic
      Games', in Fernandez Peña, Cerezuela, Gómez Benosa, Kennett,
      and de Moragas Spà (eds) *An Olympic Mosaic: Multidisciplinary
      Research and Dissemination of Olympic Studies* (Centre d'Estudis
      Olímpics, 2009), pp 211–31.

130   Brunet, 'Analysis of the Economic Impact of the Olympics Games',
      p 222.

131   Jules Boykoff and Gilmar Mascarenhas, 'The Olympics,
      Sustainability, and Greenwashing: The Rio 2016 Summer Games',
      Capitalism Nature Socialism 27 (2016), pp 1–11.

132   Jon Helge Lesjø, 'Lillehammer 1994: Planning, Figurations and the
      "Green" Winter Games', *International Review for the Sociology of
      Sport* 35 (2000), pp 282–93.

133   Glenn Collins, 'Coke's Hometown Olympics'; *New York Times*,
      28 March 1996, p D1.

134   Charles Rutheiser, *Imagineering Atlanta: The Politics of Place
      in the City of Dreams* (Verso, 1996), p 178; Center on Housing
      Rights and Evictions (COHRE), 'Atlanta's Olympic Legacy', 2007;

Larry Keating and Carol A. Flores, 'Sixty and Out: Techwood Homes Transformed by Enemies and Friends', *Journal of Urban History* 26 (2000), pp 275–311.

135   COHRE, 'Atlanta's Olympic Legacy', p 5.

136   COHRE, 'Atlanta's Olympic Legacy', p 32.

137   Shaila Dewan, 'Bomber Offers Guilty Pleas, and Defiance', *New York Times*, 14 April 2005, p A2.

138   Jere Longman, 'Female Athletes and Africans New Stars', *New York Times*, 5 August 1996, p A1.

139   Thomas A. Hamilton, 'The Long Hard Fall from Mount Olympus: The 2002 Salt Lake City Olympic Games Bribery Scandal', *Marquette Sports Law Review* 21 (2010), p 223.

140   Sydney Organising Committee for the Olympic Games, 'Official Report of the XXVII Olympiad, Vol. 1, Preparing for the Games', 2001, p 352.

141   Sydney Organising Committee for the Olympic Games, 'Official Report of the XXVII Olympiad', pp 352–63.

142   John Shaw, 'The Budget and the Public Nag', *New York Times*, 10 May 1999, p D4.

143   Helen Jefferson Lenskyj, *The Best Olympics Ever? Social Impacts of Sydney 2000* (State University of New York Press, 2002), p 197.

144   Miller, *The Official History of the Olympic Games and the IOC*, p 338.

145   'After Sydney Burned Bright, Athens Comes Under Fire', *Washington Post*, 3 October 2000, p D2.

Chapter 3

1   Rebecca R. Ruiz and Michael Schwirtz, 'Russian Insider Says State-Run Doping Fueled Olympic Gold', *New York Times*, 12 May 2016.

2   Jerry Brewer, 'Leaders Hail the Power of the Games: It's Time to Use it for Some Good', *Washington Post*, 19 February 2022.

3   Robert Christison, 'Observations on the Effects of Cuca, or Coca, the Leaves of Erythroxylon Coca', *British Medical Journal* 1 (1976), p 527, p 530.

4   Paul Dimeo, *A History of Drug Use in Sport 1876–1976: Beyond Good and Evil* (Routledge, 2007), p 9.

5   Paul Dimeo and Thomas M. Hunt, 'The Doping of Athletes in Former East Germany: A Critical Assessment of Comparisons with Nazi Medical Experiments', *International Review for the Sociology of Sport* 47 (2011), pp 581–93.

6   Quoted in Thomas M. Hunt, *Drug Games: The International Olympic Committee and the Politics of Doping* (University of Texas Press, 2011), p 9.

7   Dimeo, *A History of Drug Use in Sport 1876–1976*; Hunt, *Drug Games*.

8   Quoted in Hunt, *Drug Games*, p 41.

9   Hunt, *Drug Games*, p 71.

10 Duncan Mackay, 'Sir Craig Reedie Reveals in New Book How Russian Spies and Thomas Bach Were Out to Get Him', *Inside the Games*, 16 July 2022.

11 Hunt, *Drug Games*, p 136.

12 Jules Boykoff, 'A Bid for a Better Olympics', *New York Times*, 13 August 2014.

13 Bent Flyvbjerg, Alexander Budzier, and Daniel Lunn, 'Regression to the Tail: Why the Olympics Blow Up', *Environment and Planning A: Economy and Space* 53 (2021), pp 233–60.

14 Jules Boykoff, *Power Games: A Political History of the Olympics* (Verso, 2016), p 215.

15 Samantha Raphelson, 'South Korea Prepares to Spend $13 Billion on Winter Olympics. Is It Worth It?' *NPR*, 2 February 2018.

16 Jack Gallagher, 'Japanese Athletes Being Drawn into Expanding Battle over Tokyo Olympics', *CBC*, 18 May 2021; Stephen Wade, 'Tokyo's Delayed Olympics: Who Pays Bills for Another Year?', Associated Press, 25 March 2020.

17 Flyvbjerg et al, 'Regression to the Tail'.

18 Kim Tong-Hyung and Stephen Wade, 'Pyeongchang Olympics: Costly Venues May Eventually be Razed', *Associated Press*, 19 September 2018.

19 Steven Bloor, 'Abandoned Athens Olympic 2004 Venues, 10 Years On – In Pictures', *Guardian*, 13 August 2014.

20 Claire Provost and Simone Lai, 'Occupy Turin: Refugees Find a Home in Italy's Abandoned Olympic Village', *Guardian*, 2 March 2016; 'Turin's Olympic Village Houses Migrants', *Reuters*, 25 January 2018.

21 'Tokyo Olympics Report Hardly Goes Down in History as an "Asset"', *Asahi Shimbun*, 27 June 2022.

22 Steve Chiotakis, 'What LA 2028 Can Learn from Tokyo Games: Politics, Costs, Climate Change, and More', *KCRW*, 9 August 2021.

23 David Wharton, 'Estimated Cost of 2028 Los Angeles Olympics Jumps to $6.9 Billion', *Los Angeles Times*, 30 April 2019.

24 Ania Nussbaum, 'Macron's $8.5 Billion Olympics Is Already Facing Soaring Costs', *Bloomberg*, 25 July 2022.

25 Centre on Housing Rights and Evictions (COHRE), 'One World, Whose Dream? Housing Rights Violations and the Beijing Olympic Games', Geneva, July 2008, p 8.

26 Anne-Marie Brady, 'The Beijing Olympics as a Campaign of Mass Distraction', *China Quarterly* 197 (2009), pp 18–19.

27 COHRE, 'One World, Whose Dream?', p 6.

28 Maureen Fan, 'China Defends Relocation Policy', *Washington Post*, 20 February 2008.

29 Sebastian Coe, 'It's Ludicrous to Claim the Olympics Will Lead to Evictions and Poverty', *Guardian*, 14 June 2007.

30 Oliver Wainwright, '"A Massive Betrayal": How London's Olympic Legacy Was Sold Out', *Guardian*, 30 June 2022.

31 Aurelia Foster, 'London Olympics: Residents "Betrayed" Over Housing Promise', *BBC*, 20 July 2022.

32 Tom Horton, 'House Prices in Newham "Rising Faster than Anywhere in London"', *Newham Recorder*, 4 January 2018.

33 Olivia Tobin, 'Revealed: The London Boroughs with the Highest Rates of Homelessness in England', *Evening Standard*, 22 November 2018.

34 Sanne Derks, Martijn Koster, and Martijn Oosterbaan, 'Olympic Legacies', *City & Society* 32 (2020), p 189.

35 Jules Boykoff, *NOlympians: Inside the Fight Against Capitalist Mega-Sports in Los Angeles, Tokyo, and Beyond* (Fernwood Publishing, 2020), pp 21–2.

36 Kosuke Inagaki, '聖火は照らす ＴＯＫＹＯ２０２０）第４部：１ 神宮外苑、高層化なし崩し' ('Torch Illuminates Tokyo 2020: Part 4, Jingu Gaien, No Rise in Height', *Asahi Shimbun*, 25 July 2019; '五輪疑惑で注目集める竹田恒和元JOC会長," ニュースサイト' (Former JOC President Tsunekazu Takeda in the Spotlight Amid Olympics Scandal,'), *Hunter Investigative Journalism*, 3 November 2022.

37 Ruairidh Villar and Hyun Oh, 'Tokyo Man to Lose Home to Make Way for Stadium: Again', *Reuters*, 19 September 2013; Dave Zirin and Jules Boykoff, 'These Women Have Lost Their Homes to the Olympics in Tokyo – Twice', *The Nation*, 23 July 2019.

38 Minas Samatas, 'Security and Surveillance in the Athens 2004 Olympics: Some Lessons from a Troubled Story', *International Criminal Justice Review* 17 (2007), p 225.

39 John Sugden, 'Watched by the Games: Surveillance and Security
    at the Olympics', in Sugden and Tomlinson (eds) *Watching the
    Olympics: Politics, Power and Representation* (Routledge, 2012),
    pp 231–2; Jean-Loup Chappelet and Brenda Kübler-Mabbott, *The
    International Olympic Committee and the Olympic System: The
    Governance of World Sport* (Routledge, 2008), p 46.
40 Samatas, 'Security and Surveillance in the Athens 2004 Olympics',
    p 224.
41 George Floridis, 'Security for the 2004 Athens Olympic Games',
    Mediterranean Quarterly 15 (2004), p 5.
42 'Vancouver Police Get Sonic Crowd Control Device', *CBC News*,
    10 November 2009.
43 Ian Austen, 'Security at the Games and Its Cost Are Heavy', *New
    York Times*, 18 February 2010.
44 Personal interview, 18 August 2010.
45 Austen, 'Security at the Games and Its Cost Are Heavy'; Darryl
    Plecas, Martha Dow, Jordan Diplock, and John Martin, 'The
    Planning and Execution of Security for the 2010 Winter Olympic
    Games: 38 Best Practices and Lessons Learned', Center for Public
    Safety and Criminal Justice Research, 2011, pp 1–48.
46 Marsha Lederman, 'Vancouver Orders Removal of Anti-Olympic
    Mural', *The Globe and Mail*, 11 December 2009.
47 Jules Boykoff, 'The Anti-Olympics', *New Left Review* 67 (2011),
    pp 41–59.
48 Boykoff, *Power Games*.
49 Rio de Janeiro 2015 Candidate City Bid, Volume 3, 2009 p 33.
50 Justin McCurry, 'Japan Passes "Brutal" Counter-Terror Law
    Despite Fears Over Civil Liberties', *Guardian*, 15 July 2017.
51 Layla Foroudi, 'France Looks to AI-powered Surveillance to Secure
    Olympics', *Reuters*, 23 March 2023; Lisa O'Carroll, 'French
    Court's Approval of Olympics AI Surveillance Plan Fuels Privacy
    Concerns', *Guardian*, 18 May 2023.
52 Jules Boykoff and Gilmar Mascarenhas, 'The Olympics,
    Sustainability, and Greenwashing: The Rio 2016 Summer Games',
    Capitalism Nature Socialism 27 (2016), pp 1–11.
53 Christine M. O'Bonsawin, 'Showdown at Eagleridge Bluffs:
    The 2010 Vancouver Olympic Winter Games, the Olympic
    Sustainability Smokescreen, and the Protection of Indigenous
    Lands', in Forsyth, O'Bonsawin, and Heine (eds) *Intersections and
    Intersectionalities in Olympic and Paralympic Studies: Twelfth
    International Symposium for Olympic Research*, International

Centre for Olympic Studies, Western University, London, Ontario, Canada (2014), pp 82–88.

54 Martin Müller, Sven Daniel Wolfe, Christopher Gaffney, David Gogishvili, Miriam Hug, and Annick Leick, 'An Evaluation of the Sustainability of the Olympic Games', *Nature Sustainability* 4 (2021), p 342.

55 Müller et al, 'An Evaluation of the Sustainability of the Olympic Games', pp 340–8.

56 International Olympic Committee, 'UN General Assembly Recognises that "the Unifying and Conciliative Nature" of Major International Sports Events "Should Be Respected"', 1 December 2022. Also see: United Nations General Assembly, 'Sport as an Enabler of Sustainable Development', 77th session, 1 December 2022, pp 1–9.

57 Martin Müller, '(Im-)Mobile Policies: Why Sustainability Went Wrong in the 2014 Olympics in Sochi', *European Urban and Regional Studies* 22 (2015), p 206.

58 Jules Boykoff, *Celebration Capitalism and the Olympic Games* (Routledge, 2013), pp 76–9.

59 Jules Boykoff, *Activism and the Olympics: Dissent at the Games in Vancouver and London* (Rutgers University Press, 2014), pp 102–3.

60 Müller, '(Im-)Mobile Policies', pp 191–209.

61 Boykoff and Mascarenhas, 'The Olympics, Sustainability, and Greenwashing', pp 5–6; Jules Boykoff, 'What Makes Brazilians Sick', *New York Times*, 18 July 2016.

62 Rebecca Kim, 'They Went and Did It: 500-year-old Primeval Forest at Mount Gariwang Unlawfully Destroyed for 2018 Pyeongchang Winter Olympics', *Games Monitor*, 22 November 2014.

63 Jung Woo Lee, 'A Thin Line between a Sport Mega-event and a Mega-construction Project: The 2018 Winter Olympic Games in PyeongChang and its Event-led Development', *Managing Sport and Leisure* 26 (2021), p 402 (emphasis added), p 408.

64 David Cyranoski, 'Chinese Biologists Lead Outcry Over Winter Olympics Ski Site', *Nature* 524 (2015), pp 278–9.

65 Derek Van Dam, 'All the Beijing Snow Is Human-Made: A Resource-Intensive, "Dangerous" Trend as Planet Warms', *CNN*, 5 February 2022.

66 Jules Boykoff and Dave Zirin, 'Tokyo's 2020 Olympics Are Showing the Nightmare Waiting for LA in 2028', *Los Angeles Times*, 23 July 2019.

67 Koide Hiroaki, 'The Fukushima Nuclear Disaster and the Tokyo Olympics', *The Asia-Pacific Journal* 18 (2020), p 4.

68 Dave Zirin and Jules Boykoff, 'Is Fukushima Safe for the Olympics?' *The Nation*, 25 July 2019.

69 Jane Braxton Little, 'Fukushima Residents Return Despite Radiation', *Scientific American*, 16 January 2019.

70 Taro Kotegawa, 'Bags of Debris from Fukushima Disaster Swept Away in Typhoon', *Asahi Shimbun*, 14 October 2019.

71 Ryan Holifield and Mick Day, 'A Framework for a Critical Physical Geography of "Sacrifice Zones": Physical Landscapes and Discursive Spaces of Frac Sand Mining in Western Wisconsin', *Geoforum* 85 (2017), pp 269–79.

72 Jules Boykoff and Christopher Gaffney, 'The Tokyo 2020 Games and the End of Olympic History', *Capitalism Nature Socialism* 31 (2020), pp 1–19.

73 Rainforest Action Network, 'Broken Promises: A Case Study on How the Tokyo 2020 Games and Japanese Financiers Are Fueling Land-Grabbing and Rainforest Destruction in Indonesia', November 2018; Rainforest Action Network, 'NGO Statement of Concern on Tokyo 2020 Olympics' Revised Timber Sourcing Code', 30 January 2019.

74 Rainforest Action Network, 'Joint NGO Statement on Tokyo 2020 Olympics' "Fake Sustainability"', https://www.ran.org/press-releases/olympics-fake-sustainability/

75 Boykoff and Gaffney, 'Tokyo 2020 and the End of Olympic History'.

76 Boykoff, *NOlympians*, pp 39–40.

77 International Olympic Committee, 'Host City Contract Principles: Games of the XXXIV Olympiad in 2028', 13 September 2017, p 10.

78 Jules Boykoff, 'Toward a Theory of Sportswashing: Mega-Events, Soft Power, and Political Conflict', *Sociology of Sport Journal* 39 (2022), pp 342–51.

79 Jules Boykoff, 'The World Is Sliding Toward Authoritarianism. So Are the Olympics', *Politico*, 7 February 2022.

80 Andrew Keh, 'Power Game: Thomas Bach's Iron Grip on the Olympics', *New York Times*, 20 July 2021.

81 Antoni Slodkowski, Nathan Layne, Mari Saito, and Ami Miyazaki, 'Japan Businessman Paid $8.2 Million by Tokyo Olympics Bid Lobbied Figure at Center of French Corruption Probe', *Reuters*, 30 March 2020.

82   Dave Zirin and Jules Boykoff, 'A Bribery Scandal Hits the "2020" Tokyo Olympics', *The Nation*, 1 April 2020.

83   Justin McCurry, 'Tokyo Olympics Bribery Scandal Threatens to Derail Winter Games Bid', *Guardian*, 6 December 2022; Anthony Kuhn, 'A Corruption Scandal Has Added a Dark Footnote to the Tokyo Olympics', *NPR*, 29 October 2022.

84   Dave Zirin and Jules Boykoff, 'The Paris Olympics Are Developing a Familiar Stench', *The Nation*, 27 June 2023.

85   Andrew Jennings, 'The Love That Dare Not Speak Its Name: Corruption and the Olympics', in Lenskyj and Wagg (eds) *The Palgrave Handbook of Olympic Studies* (Palgrave Macmillan, 2012), p 469. Jennings' mafia description comes from Neeraj Kumar.

86   'Brazil's Nuzman Sentenced to 30 Years in Jail for Rio 2016 Corruption', *Reuters*, 26 November 2021.

87   Rob Nixon, *Slow Violence and the Environmentalism of the Poor* (Harvard University Press, 2011), p 2.

88   Boykoff, *NOlympians*.

89   See: https://counterolympicsnetwork.wordpress.com/ and http://www.gamesmonitor.org.uk/

90   William Andrews, 'Playful Protests and Contested Urban Space: The 2020 Tokyo Olympics Protest Movement', *The Asia-Pacific Journal* 18 (2020), pp 1–11.

91   Dave Zirin and Jules Boykoff, 'The Tokyo 2020 Olympics Are Likely to Be a Disaster', *The Nation*, 22 July 2019.

92   Jules Boykoff, 'The Olympics Are Globally Mobile. Now the Anti-Olympics Movement Is Too', *Jacobin*, 24 May 2022.

93   Personal interview, 14 May 2020.

Chapter 4

1   'IOC President Thomas Bach Makes Final Plea to Support Much-Needed Changes to Keep Olympic Games Relevant', *Associated Press*, 7 December 2014.

2   Dennis Pauschinger and John Lauermann, 'Civil Society, Contestation, and the Games', *Play the Game*, 8 October 2018.

3   'Thomas Bach Elected IOC President', *Associated Press*, 10 September 2013.

4   Thomas Bach, 'New Year's Message 2020', *International Olympic Committee*, 1 January 2020.

5   Christine Brennan, 'IOC President Thomas Bach Isn't Fit to Lead', *USA Today*, 3 February 2022.

6 Geoff Berkeley, 'Bach Issues Warning to Athletes Who Support Russian Invasion of Ukraine', *Inside the Games*, 20 May 2022.

7 International Olympic Committee, 'Statement on Solidarity with Ukraine, Sanctions against Russia and Belarus, and the Status of Athletes from these Countries', 25 January 2023.

8 International Olympic Committee, *Olympic Charter*, Lausanne, Switzerland, 8 August 2021, p 8.

9 Susannah Walden, 'Kyiv Calls International Olympic Committee "Promoter of War"', *AFP*, 30 January 2023.

10 Theodor Adorno, 'Commitment', in Bloch, Lukács, Brecht, Benjamin, and Adorno, *Aesthetics and Politics* (Verso, 1980), p 177.

11 International Olympic Committee, 'Olympic Agenda 2020: 20+20 Recommendations', December 2014, pp 1–25.

12 Executive Steering Committee for Olympic Games Delivery, 'Olympic Games: The New Norm', International Olympic Committee, February 2018, pp 1–58.

13 Sven Daniel Wolfe, 'Building a Better Host City? Reforming and Contesting the Olympics in Paris 2024', *Environment and Planning C: Politics and Space* 41 (2022), p 264.

14 See, for example: Executive Steering Committee for Olympic Games Delivery, 'Olympic Games: The New Norm', pp 1–58.

15 Wolfe, 'Building a Better Host City?', p 264.

16 International Olympic Committee, 'Future Host Commissions: Terms of Reference', 3 October 2019, p 4.

17 International Olympic Committee, 'Future Host Commissions', p 5.

18 David Jancsics, 'Corruption as Resource Transfer: An Interdisciplinary Synthesis', *Public Administration Review* 70 (2019), p 530.

19 David Owen, 'Agenda 2020: The Sequel', *Inside the Games*, 17 February 2021.

20 Thomas Bach, '137th IOC Session: Olympic Agenda 2020 Closing Report', 10 March 2021, p 13.

21 Wolfe, 'Building a Better Host City?', p 258, p 269.

22 International Olympic Committee, 'Ethics', September 2022, https://stillmed.olympics.com/media/Document%20Library/OlympicOrg/Documents/Code-of-Ethics/Code-of-Ethics-ENG.pdf

23 Matthew Campelli, 'Is It Time for a Climate Regulator in Sport?', *The Sustainability Report*, 9 March 2023.

24   David Owen, 'The Most Important IOC Member in History Not to
      Have Been Made President Prepares to Move Upstairs', *Inside the
      Games*, 25 December 2022.
25   Owen, 'The Most Important IOC Member in History'.
26   Jules Boykoff, *Power Games: A Political History of the Olympics*
      (Verso, 2016), pp 163–8.
27   Jill Martin, 'Georgia Dome Imploded After 25 Years of Use', *CNN*,
      20 November 2017.
28   Walker J. Ross and Madeleine Orr, 'Predicting Climate Impacts
      to the Olympic Games and FIFA Men's World Cups from 2022
      to 2032', *Sport in Society* 25 (2022), pp 867–88; Daniel Scott,
      Robert Steiger, Michelle Rutty, and Peter Johnson, 'The Future of
      the Olympic Winter Games in an Era of Climate Change', *Current
      Issues in Tourism* 18 (2015), pp 913–30.
29   International Olympic Committee, *Olympic Charter*, Lausanne,
      Switzerland, 8 August 2021, p 8.
30   Christopher Bodeen, 'Samaranch Approves Beijing's Environmental
      Outlook for 2022', Associated Press, 18 September 2018.
31   Personal interview, 13 February 2023.
32   Personal interview, 13 February 2023.
33   Human Rights Watch, 'Olympic Congress: Monitor Host Countries
      on Rights', 1 October 2009.
34   International Olympic Committee, 'IOC Strategic Framework on
      Human Rights', September 2022, p 45, p 8. Also see pp 30–3.
35   International Olympic Committee, 'Olympic Charter Amendments
      Approved by 141st IOC Session', 15 October 2023.
36   Sven Daniel Wolfe, 'Updating the Olympic Charter Is a Dangerous
      Game', *Inside the Games*, 23 September 2023.
37   Personal interview, 13 February 2023.
38   Barbara J. Keys, 'The Ideals of International Sport', in Keys (ed)
      The Morality of Global Sport: From Peace to Human Rights
      (University of Pennsylvania Press, 2019), p 1.
39   United Nations General Assembly, Human Rights Council,
      'Promoting Human Rights through Sport and the Olympic Ideal',
      3 October 2014, https://www.icsspe.org/system/files/UN%20
      %28HCR_RES_27_8%29%20Promoting%20human%20
      rights%20through%20sport%20and%20the%20Olympic%20
      ideal.pdf
40   International Olympic Committee, *Olympic Charter*, Lausanne,
      Switzerland, 8 July 2011, p 11, emphasis added.

41 International Olympic Committee, *Olympic Charter*, Lausanne, Switzerland, 9 October 2018, p 11, emphasis added.

42 Barbara J. Keys and Roland Burke, 'The Future of Idealism in Sport', in Keys (ed) *The Morality of Global Sport: From Peace to Human Rights* (University of Pennsylvania Press, 2019), p 221, p 222.

43 Stephen Wade, 'IOC Human Rights Advisory Committee to Start with 2024 Games', Associated Press, 1 December 2018.

44 Human Rights Watch, 'Olympics: Host City Contract Requires Human Rights', 28 February 2017.

45 Personal interview, 13 February 2023.

46 Personal interview, 13 February 2023.

47 Personal interview, 13 February 2023.

48 Personal interview, 13 February 2023.

49 Personal interview, 13 February 2023.

50 Personal interview, 20 February 2023. For more information on Global Athlete, see: https://www.globalathlete.org

51 'Raven Saunders Throws Up X on Podium to Represent Where the "Oppressed Meet"', *Guardian*, 1 August 2021.

52 International Olympic Committee, *Olympic Charter*, Lausanne, Switzerland, 8 August 2021, p 14, p 94.

53, United Nations, 'The Universal Declaration of Human Rights', 10 December 1948, www.un.org/en/universal-declaration-human-rights/

54 International Olympic Committee, 'IOC Extends Opportunities for Athlete Expression During the Olympic Games Tokyo 2020', 2 July 2021.

55 Dave Zirin and Jules Boykoff, 'Despite the Ban, Protest Emerges at the Olympics', *The Nation*, 10 August 2021.

56 Personal interview, 20 February 2023.

57 Personal interview, 13 February 2023.

58 Personal interview, 20 February 2023.

59 Personal interview, 13 February 2023, emphasis added.

60 Nick Butler, 'Bach Accuses Critics of Olympic Movement of Ignorance and Aggression', *Inside the Games*, 2 November 2017.

61 April Henning and Paul Dimeo, *Doping: A Sporting History* (Reaktion Books, 2022), p 206, p 207.

62 Personal interview, 20 February 2023.

63 Pierre de Coubertin, *Olympism: Selected Writings*, Norbert Müller (ed) (International Olympic Committee, 2000), p 587.

64   Avery Brundage, 'Memos, Notes, etc.', 18 March 1950, Avery Brundage Collection (ABC), Box 245, Reel 142, International Centre for Olympic Studies (ICOS), London, Ontario.

65   'Proclamation of Opening by the Head of the Spanish State, Generalissimo Franco' and 'Address by President Avery Brundage to 63rd Session of the IOC', *Bulletin of the International Olympic Committee* (1965), pp 64–6.

66   Vyv Simson and Andrew Jennings, *The Lords of the Rings: Power, Money and Drugs in the Modern Olympics* (Simon & Schuster, 1992), p 59.

67   Pauschinger and Lauermann, 'Civil Society, Contestation, and the Games'.

68   'Vancouver Voters Back Bid for the Olympics', *New York Times*, 24 February 2003.

69   Helen Jefferson Lenskyj, *Olympic Industry Resistance: Challenging Olympic Power and Propaganda* (State University of New York Press, 2008), p 65.

70   International Olympic Committee, 'Future Host Commissions: Terms of Reference', 3 October 2019, p 4.

71   Patrick Burke, 'Barrett Extols IOC's New Process for Electing Olympic Games Hosts', *Inside the Games*, 23 May 2022.

72   International Olympic Committee, 'Future Olympic Games Elections to Be More Flexible', 22 May 2019.

73   Dave Zirin and Jules Boykoff, 'The IOC Says the 2032 Olympics Are Coming to Brisbane', *The Nation*, 16 June 2021.

74   Jules Boykoff, 'Tokyo's Olympics Have Turned Nightmarish. L.A., Are You Watching?' *Los Angeles Times*, 22 July 2021.

75   Yi-Fu Tuan, *The Good Life* (University of Wisconsin Press, 1986), p 15.

76   International Olympic Committee, *Olympic Charter*, Lausanne, Switzerland, 8 August 2021, p 8.

77   Rick Cole, 'The Global Brand: An Appreciation of the Olympic Rings', *Smith Communication Partners*, 21 July 2021.

78   Martin Luther King, Jr., 'The Death of Evil upon the Seashore,' Cathedral of St John the Divine, New York City, 17 May 1956.

FURTHER READING

International Olympic Committee and its leaders

Jean-Loup Chappelet and Brenda Kübler-Mabbott, *The International Olympic Committee and the Olympic System: The Governance of World Sport* (Routledge, 2008)

Pierre de Coubertin, *Olympism: Selected Writings* (International Olympic Committee, 2000)

Allen Guttmann, *The Games Must Go On: Avery Brundage and the Olympic Movement* (Columbia University Press, 1984)

John Horne and Garry Whannel, *Understanding the Olympics* (Routledge, 2012)

John J. MacAloon, *This Great Symbol: Pierre de Coubertin and the Origins of the Modern Olympics* (Routledge, 2008)

Olympic history

Robert K. Barney, Stephen R. Wenn, and Scott G. Martyn, *Selling the Five Rings: The International Olympic Committee and the Rise of Olympic Commercialism* (University of Utah Press, 2004)

Jules Boykoff, *Power Games: A Political History of the Olympics* (Verso, 2016)

David Goldblatt, *The Games: A Global History of the Olympics* (WW Norton and Company, 2016)

Xu Guoqi, *Olympic Dreams: China and Sports, 1895–2008* (Harvard University Press, 2008)

David Miller, *The Official History of the Olympic Games and the IOC: Athens to London 1894 to 2012* (Mainstream Publishing Company, 2012)

Olympians

John Carlos and Dave Zirin, *The John Carlos Story: The Sports Moment that Changed the World* (Haymarket Books, 2011)

Amira Rose Davis, *'Can't Eat a Medal': The Lives and Labors of Black Women Athletes in the Age of Jim Crow* (UNC Press, 2024)

Harry Edwards, *The Revolt of the Black Athlete* (University of Illinois Press, 2017 [1969])

Mark Quinn, *The King of Spring: The Life and Times of Peter O'Connor* (The Liffey Press, 2004)

Tommie Smith and David Steele, *Silent Gesture: The Autobiography of Tommie Smith* (Temple University Press, 2007)

Wyomia Tyus and Elizabeth Terzakis, *Tigerbelle: The Wyomia Tyus Story* (Akashic Books, 2018)

Anti-Olympics activism

Adam Berg, *The Olympics That Never Happened: Denver '76 and the Politics of Growth* (University of Texas Press, 2023)

Jules Boykoff, *NOlympians: Inside the Fight Against Capitalist Mega-Sports in Los Angeles, Tokyo, and Beyond* (Fernwood, 2020)

Helen Jefferson Lenskyj, *Inside the Olympic Industry: Power, Politics, and Activism* (State University of New York Press, 2000)

Helen Jefferson Lenskyj, *Olympic Industry Resistance: Challenging Olympic Power and Propaganda* (State University of New York Press, 2008)

INDEX

References to figures are in *italics* and to tables are in **bold**; references to notes are the page number followed by the note number (129n1).